MALLARMÉ AND THE SYMBOLIST DRAMA

HASKELL M. BLOCK

Professor of Comparative Literature
Brooklyn College of the City University of New York

WAYNE STATE UNIVERSITY PRESS

DETROIT 1963

WAYNE STATE UNIVERSITY STUDY NUMBER 14

LANGUAGE AND LITERATURE

IN MEMORY OF JEAN—MARIE CARRÉ

CONTENTS

PREFACE   I

I

THE POET IN THE THEATER   5
Hérodiade and the *Faune*

II

IGITUR AND HAMLET   36

III

HOMAGE TO WAGNER   52

IV

THE VISION OF A NEW THEATER   83

V

THE EARLY SYMBOLIST DRAMA   101

VI

MALLARMÉ'S DRAMATIC HERITAGE   129

NOTES   135

BIBLIOGRAPHY   155

INDEX   161

PREFACE

THIS BOOK IS, TO THE BEST OF MY knowledge, the first detailed examination of the relationship of Mallarmé to the drama. The present study represents an effort to situate the poet's dramatic theories and aspirations within the broad context of the forces shaping the modern drama, as well as within the narrower framework of Mallarmé's literary career. My concern is at once historical and critical, for the poet's impact on the theater of the later nineteenth and the twentieth centuries cannot be separated from the intrinsic values of his theory and expression. I have undertaken this study, persuaded not only of the enduring significance of Mallarmé's art, but also of the need to understand more completely the premises and characteristics of the drama which he helped to create.

This study is the consequence of a long interest in Mallarmé and the symbolist movement on the one hand and in the development of the modern drama on the other. I have not attempted to write a detailed history of the symbolist drama; yet no discussion of Mallarmé can be divorced from larger historical considerations. It is as a part of the history and criticism of the symbolist drama, not only in France, but also throughout the Western world, that our view of Mallarmé's dramatic efforts will take on full significance. At the same time, the crisis of the theater out of which symbolist drama emerged, and which the symbolists vainly sought to resolve, has not diminished in the more than half a century since Mallarmé's death. It is my hope that this study will help to illuminate some of the con-

I

tinuing tensions and conflicting values in the theater of our own day as well as of an earlier time.

It should not be necessary to point out that a discussion of a writer and his art presupposes a belief in their significance. I should not wish to imply that I consider Mallarmé's dramatic theory and compositions the most important single part of his achievement or that I regard the symbolist drama as the only significant mode of dramatic expression. Nonetheless, our understanding of other writers and their works and other tendencies and movements in the modern theater: naturalism, expressionism, social realism, existentialism, and the like, far exceeds our awareness and comprehension of the role of the symbolist poets and playwrights. With due regard to proportion, we should make the effort to understand all of the impulses shaping the theater in our time, from an historical and critical standpoint and with an attitude of imaginative sympathy.

I am indebted to many scholars and critics who have helped to make this work possible. I feel a deep sense of gratitude to John Gassner, whose writings have repeatedly broken new ground in the interpretation of the modern drama. I am grateful too to Wallace Fowlie and Robert Greer Cohn for their thoughtful reading of the manuscript and their helpful suggestions. My colleague, William T. Bandy, generously supplied me with copies of unpublished letters of Mallarmé concerning some of his dramatic projects. Specific acknowledgment to individual authors will be found in the notes and bibliography, but I should like to record my keen sense of obligation to the late Henri Mondor, without whose labors this book would not have been possible.

A portion of the first chapter appears in somewhat different form, entitled "Dramatic Values in Mallarmé's *Hérodiade*," in *Stil- und Formprobleme in der Literatur* (Copyright 1959. Carl Winter, Universitätsverlag, Heidelberg). The permission of the publisher to reproduce this material is acknowledged with thanks.

I am happy to record my gratitude to the Oslo Kommunes Kunstsamlinger and its Director, Johan H. Langaard, for authorization to reproduce the lithographic portrait of Mallarmé by Edvard Munch on the jacket cover. The reproduction is from a photograph kindly supplied by O. Væring, Oslo.

I am grateful to the Research Committee of the Graduate School and to Dean Mark H. Ingraham of the College of Letters and Science, the University of Wisconsin, for a leave of absence which enabled me to complete the research for this study. The Memorial Library of the University of Wisconsin kindly obtained many of the secondary materials through interlibrary loans. I deeply appreciate the generous cooperation and aid provided by Harold A. Basilius, Director of the Wayne State University Press, and Patricia Davis, Editor. I should also like to express my thanks to friends and colleagues who encouraged my efforts, and especially to my wife, Elaine, for her affectionate help.

H. M. B.
Brooklyn, New York

I

THE POET IN THE THEATER

Hérodiade and the *Faune*

WITH THE PASSAGE OF TIME THE GREATNESS of the poetry of Mallarmé has become more and more apparent. The publication of scores of volumes of collected writings, letters, texts, biographical and critical interpretations serves to call attention to the enduring significance of the poet's art. Mallarmé's achievement resides not only in the intrinsic richness and vitality of his poems, but also in the continuity of theory and expression since his time which testifies to his central role among the makers of modern literature.

No adequate account of the forms and styles of modern drama can fail to take into account the contribution of the symbolist poets and playwrights; yet the role of Mallarmé in shaping this important area of dramatic theory and technique has been virtually ignored. To appreciate Mallarmé's deep involvement in the theater and his impact on European drama at the end of the nineteenth century, we must examine the ways in which his lifelong theatrical aspirations found expression. Our understanding of the symbolist drama—its values and limitations, its accomplishments and failures—depends first of all on our appreciation of Mallarmé's endeavors, for symbolist drama, like symbolist poetry, is to a considerable extent the creation of the author of *Hérodiade*.

We surely would not include Mallarmé among the great playwrights of the later nineteenth century, and yet, without his example and inspiration, it is doubtful that either symbolist drama or symbolist poetry would have come into being. Today, no one would question the centrality of Mallarmé as the great poet of the symbolist movement. Albert Thibaudet in his masterful study of the poet declares: "*nul mieux que Mallarmé, par la nature de son génie et par le sens de son art, ne fut authentiquement un symboliste.*"[1] In his preoccupation with the mystery of the universe which only the poet can reveal, through his perception of analogies and correspondences between the visible and invisible realms of being, Mallarmé is the great synthesizer of symbolist thought and expression. The object of the poet, he asserts, is to seize "*les rapports, entre temps, rares ou multipliés; d'après quelque état intérieur*" (647).[2] The moods or inner feelings which the poet re-creates in his verse can be suggested or reflected only by means of the magical and evocative properties of language: hence, Mallarmé's life-long obsession with the mystery of poetic language, with the demon of analogy, and with the music of silence.

It is not easy to see in this difficult and withdrawn poet the figure of a dramatist, but any overall view of Mallarmé's development must consider his continuous and intimate affiliation with the theater.[3] A love of performance seems to have been instinctive in the poet as a boy; for himself as well as for his family at Sens, Mallarmé at the age of sixteen and seventeen performed spectacles in which he played all the parts on an improvised "stage."[4] In his early, unpublished compositions, dramatic elements fuse with the poet's lyrical expression. "*Loeda: Idylle antique*," dated April 1859, is a dramatic poem in the classical tradition which retells the story of Leda and the swan.[5] Inspired perhaps by Leconte de Lisle as well as by Chénier,[6] it is an early anticipation of "*L'Après-midi d'un Faune*," not only in mood and development, but also in direct allusion:[7]

> Effleurant le gazon de mille pieds d'albâtre,
> Les nymphes en riant fuient un faune lascif.

"*Loeda*" may well mark the beginning of the dramatic poem of 1865.

There are other indications of the young Mallarmé's deep interest in the drama. His first publications, only recently discovered, were two theatrical chronicles published in the journal, *Le Sénonais*, in 1861.[8] When these early drama reviews are published, it will be interesting to see what awareness they reveal of the theater's ways and means. Although his early interest in the theater was genuine, poetry was Mallarmé's first love, and his subsequent efforts toward a fusion of poetry and drama are undoubtedly a response to such diverse influences as Shakespeare, Goethe, Hugo, Banville, Glatigny, and Villiers de l'Isle-Adam. From the beginning of his career, Mallarmé was intensely aware of the dramatic element in poetry. Of his early poem, "*L'Azur*," he declared, "*il y a là un vrai drame.*"[9] Even before his enfranchisement from the idiom of Baudelaire, he experienced the conflict of the actual and the ideal as an inherently dramatic quality of his poetry.[10] His early reading of both French classical and foreign drama familiarized him with the ways in which poetry had found expression in the great drama of the past, and it is altogether understandable why Mallarmé at Tournon, despite his isolation from great centers of theatrical activity, should have turned to the drama for his principal literary efforts.

Mallarmé's major dramatic compositions date from 1864, his twenty-second year. The possibility of a literary drama was suggested to him not only by his reading of Musset,[11] and his absorption with the verse drama of Banville, but also by his meeting with Villiers de l'Isle-Adam in 1863,[12] at a moment when Villiers was preoccupied with his vast dramatic projects. It is difficult to say precisely what inspired Mallarmé in 1864 to compose his *Hérodiade*, but there can be no doubt that the high purpose animating the dramatic ambitions of Banville and Villiers spurred him in the direction of the theater.

In the spring of 1864 Mallarmé gave eloquent proof, in his "*Symphonie Littéraire*," of his admiration for Théodore de Banville. Mallarmé's attachment to Banville dates perhaps from

7

1860—at the very beginning of his dedication to poetry.[13] In "*Symphonie Littéraire*," Banville is no ordinary poet, "*mais la voix même de la lyre*" (264). His musicality, grace, lyricism, and magic endeared him to his young disciple. Much later, in a memorial essay of 1892, Mallarmé expressed his old admiration for Banville simply and directly: "*je vouai à Théodore de Banville un culte*" (520). Banville, "*musicien de mots*," was important to Mallarmé not only for his pastoral landscapes and his rich and supple command of language, but also for his "*théâtre prestigieux*" (523), a theater which Mallarmé knew and admired before he made any of his attempts at dramatic composition and a theater which he viewed, both in his youth and his maturity, as a high achievement in the art of drama.[14]

We cannot be altogether sure of the nature of the drama which Mallarmé conceived of as *Hérodiade* in 1864, but it is reasonable to suppose that the characterization and language were suggested, at least in part, by Eros' description of "*la cruelle Diane*" in Banville's *Diane au Bois* of 1863.[15] Diane's obsession with virginity, her beauty, and her remoteness are all vividly set forth:[16]

> Elle voulait s'enfuir dans les bois du Taygète,
> Et dans les antres noirs, pendant l'éternité,
> Ensevelir sa haine et sa virginité.

Similarly, Diane's fanatic cult of purity points to Mallarmé's cold heroine; in Act II of Banville's play we see her visibly torn between virginity and love, striving desperately to remain "*Pure et blanche au milieu des splendeurs virginales!*"[17] Outwardly, Mallarmé's Hérodiade has transcended the turbulence of passion; yet despite this fundamental difference, the similarities to Banville's Diane are unmistakable.

Villiers de l'Isle-Adam's novel, *Isis* (1862), is even more important as a source of the character of Hérodiade.[18] Mallarmé clearly received much from Villiers besides a propulsion toward the drama. Tullia Fabriana, heroine of *Isis*, is unusually beautiful, yet solitary, mysterious, inviolate, and unapproachable. We see her primarily through the eyes of Count de

Strally-d'Anthas, for whom she remains a cold, inaccessible beauty. Her conscious superiority to the great majority of mankind is readily apparent: "*Elle estimait son âme comme quelque chose de trop préférable à l'univers entier, pour la laisser entrevoir de personne.* ..."[19] She communes with dark powers and seems to possess secret knowledge of the mysteries of the universe. Mallarmé's drama was conceived according to the traditions of French classical tragedy; yet his heroine clearly belongs to the realm of the occult and supernatural inhabited by Tullia Fabriana.[20]

It is by no means certain that we have more than a fragment of the *Hérodiade* drama which Mallarmé began at Tournon late in 1864. Any discussion of the play must perforce embrace altogether different sections of the work, written at various stages of the poet's life. We know that at one time he planned *Hérodiade* as a three-act drama,[21] and it may well be that part or even all of the full-length play was written and then destroyed or lost. Any consideration of *Hérodiade* as a drama must be provisional; it is altogether possible that a more extensive version of the composition of 1864-65 may some day be brought to light.

In Mallarmé's career no other work has the sustained importance of *Hérodiade*. From its very inception to the end of the poet's life, he was endlessly preoccupied with its composition: his correspondence makes it plain that none of his other works cost him so much pain and effort. Unable to complete *Hérodiade*, Mallarmé was unwilling to let it go, and his inability to leave the poem alone even after he resolved to abandon it as a play is in itself proof of the power of its fascination. Unquestionably, Mallarmé's inner conflicts and crises during the early stages of the composition of *Hérodiade* were responsible for the alternating attraction and repulsion it exerted during some of his most productive years. There is no doubt that this inner stress and strain find expression in the work. Thus, in 1866 the poet wrote to Cazalis, in *Hérodiade* "*je m'étais mis tout entier sans le savoir.*"[22] However, the poet's awareness of his involvement in his poem does not authorize us to identify

9

Mallarmé and Hérodiade and to proceed to a psychoanalysis of one by means of the other. *Hérodiade* is a work far different from the sonnets and other short poems which immediately precede it in point of time; it is less personal, more intricate, more complex, and it imposes a whole new set of claims and interests on the reader's attention.

The poem as we may read it in the "Pléiade" edition of Mallarmé's *Œuvres complètes* (41-49) is in three parts: "Ouverture"; "Scène"; and "Cantique de Saint Jean." Plainly, in this form the poem is not complete, but what Mallarmé originally wrote for the work he entitled *Hérodiade* may never be fully known, nor are we better informed about the various stages of composition through which the work passed. Of the three sections, only the "Scène" appeared during Mallarmé's lifetime. It was entitled "*Fragment d'une étude scénique ancienne d'un Poëme de Hérodiade*," first published in the second volume of *Le Parnasse Contemporain*, printed in 1869 and published in 1871. Thus, only a few years after its composition, Mallarmé viewed this section of the work as a dramatic fragment. His inability to complete *Hérodiade* as a drama and his failure to achieve even the slightest theatrical success during his career have led some of his keenest interpreters to the view that drama had no place in his work. Thus, Albert Thibaudet asserted that Mallarmé was "*incapable du moindre coup de crayon dramatique*," [23] and Emilie Noulet has written of *Hérodiade*, "*du point de vue dramatique, l'œuvre n'est pas défendable*." [24] Yet, we know that Mallarmé originally conceived of *Hérodiade* as a tragedy, for he speaks of "*ma tragédie d'Hérodiade*" more than once in his letters of 1865, [25] and he went so far as to communicate his project to Théodore de Banville, who had recently achieved some success at the Théâtre Français. The older poet was glad to be of service to the young author of "*Symphonie Littéraire*," which he had seen in manuscript, [26] and he offered valuable counsel for a beginner in the theater. In his letter of March 31, 1865, Banville urged Mallarmé to prepare his drama for production in Paris:

> Je ne saurais trop vous féliciter, mon cher Ami, de l'excellente idée que vous avez de faire une *Hérodiade*, car le Théâtre-Français a justement ce qu'il faut comme décor pour la monter et ce serait une grande raison pour être reçu: ce qui généralement fait obstacle pour les pièces poétiques, c'est la crainte de dépenser de l'argent en vue d'un résultat incertain. Tâchez que l'intérêt dramatique y soit, avec la poésie, car vous feriez plus pour notre cause en continuant votre pièce de façon à ce qu'elle soit reçue et jouée, qu'en la faisant plus poétique et moins jouable. . . .[27]

There can be no doubt of the intrinsic dramatic interest of Mallarmé's subject; yet as the complexities of his conception made each step in the process of composition more difficult and painful, he was compelled to abandon the work and to take up *"un intermède héroïque, dont le héros est un Faune"* as his dramatic offering to the Théâtre Français. The meeting with Banville and Constant Coquelin in Paris in the summer of 1865 was a disaster; and when the dispirited poet returned to Tournon in the fall, he once again took up *Hérodiade, "non plus tragédie, mais poème."* [28] As a result of this new effort, no doubt, we have the "Ouverture," to which Mallarmé refers repeatedly in his letters of the following year. It should be observed, however, that his disillusionment over the failure of his attempts at stage presentation did not lead him to a total abandonment of dramatic structure; for, while the work would not be a poem or a tragedy, all of the traditional dramatic elements— *"l'attitude, les vêtements, le décor et l'ameublement, sans parler du mystère"*—would be incorporated in it. The *rapports* between poetry and drama are not as evident in the "Ouverture" as in the "Scène," but it would be altogether wrong to view the "Ouverture" simply as a poetic utterance divorced from the dramatic situation underlying the work as a whole.

From the time of its conception, Mallarmé viewed *Hérodiade* as a literary as well as a theatrical composition, and it was in the course of his meditations on *Hérodiade* that he arrived at the formulation of his revolutionary poetics: *"Peindre, non la chose, mais l'effet qu'elle produit.*" [29] The new formula was more than an echo of Poe's insistence on the primacy of emotional impact; [30] it was an injunction for the poet to go beyond the plane of descriptive or anecdotal narrative to an evocation of the subjective mood or impression that the experience of the poem induced. From this principle stems much of the conceptualization of the concrete that we find in Mallarmé's subsequent work. More than one commentator has pointed out that virtually all the lexical and syntactical complexities of Mallarmé's late poetry are present to some degree in *Hérodiade,* in the "Scène" as well as in the "Ouverture." The poet's so-called hermeticism that went hand in hand with the creation of a new poetic language may seem in itself to militate against dramatic values; yet even at the end of his career, when he had called into question the very possibility of the communicative power of poetic language, Mallarmé still thought of *Hérodiade* in part as a dramatic composition with definite scenic possibilities. [31]

The structure of the work is at once musical and dramatic. The "Ouverture," while of immense intrinsic interest, is at the same time inseparable from the "Scène" which gave rise to it and from which it derives added significance. The "Ouverture" is akin to a musical prelude in that it introduces, elaborates, and interrelates the principal themes of the work; yet it is also a dramatic monolog in which a character involved in an action presents an intimation of what will presently take place before our eyes. All is indirect and suggestive; the Nurse's incantation provides no narrative, but creates a mood of dread anticipation through a cumulative flow of images depicting the dawn. The day is dark and dreadful, fraught with fearful expectations: "*Crime! bûcher! aurore ancienne! supplice!*" The scene is one of death and desolation, of emptiness and waste, of mystery and horror. The sterility of the land, the absence of the physical processes of life, the harsh cruelty that accompanies this absence, all serve to prefigure Mallarmé's heroine before she appears. Yet, the Nurse's utterances are dark and sibylline, and she hardly knows what she is saying. She is an unconscious oracle, close enough to the events of the principal action to be able to judge them, sufficiently aware of the imminence of the terrible to wish to see it prevented: *"Car tout est présage et mauvais rêve!"* The function of the Nurse in establishing the tone and atmosphere of the scene and introducing the central character has been rightfully compared to the role of the witches in *Macbeth*.[32] The events of common life have fallen away, transformed into an inferno of stark horror colored by the red dawn of the last judgment. Viewed in intimate association with the "Scène," the "Ouverture" provides an interpretation of the heroine's behavior that helps to explain her character. Her incoherent song suggests madness; her solitary promenade, the isolation of the damned. Even more apparent is the foreshadowing and suspense which the "Ouverture" creates, the sense of dire foreboding, not only through the accumulation and juxtaposition of images, but also through the concrete evocation of scene.[33] The "Ouverture," with its striking depiction of tower, palace, garden, dawn, and the entire physical as well as spiritual environment, is as challenging an invitation to imaginative scene design as one can find anywhere, and it is tempting to wonder what an artist of kindred spirit— an Appia or a Gordon Craig—would have made of it.

If the "Ouverture" is essentially suggestion and implication,[34] the "Scène" provides the very substance of drama, through the projection and illumination of character in action. The Nurse's first words jolt us to attention by their sudden urgency: *"Tu vis! ou vois-je ici l'ombre d'une princesse?"* And at once she seeks to recall Hérodiade to a passionate participation in life. We can imagine her rushing toward the princess, only to be brutally and coldly repelled. Hérodiade's first word, *"Reculez,"* dominates all that follows in the interplay of the central characters. *"Ce cri est de fort bon théâtre,"* a perceptive drama critic has declared;[35] at once, Mallarmé fuses action and gesture, revealing a cleavage that deepens as the scene progresses: the Nurse seeking to draw Hérodiade into common, shared experience; Hérodiade asserting her isolation and inviolability as the very condition of her existence. We

13

must envision Hérodiade as supremely beautiful. The Nurse's futile attempts to decorate this beauty in ways that are humanly attractive provide objective confirmation of Hérodiade's self-description. Such dazzling beauty is death because it removes its possessor completely from the life of ordinary mortals, makes her dead-in-life and seals off the possibility of contact between her and others. Her beauty belongs to her alone; it is the source of her conscious particularity and of a superiority to others that makes her feel akin to the gods. To the Nurse, this austere and unnatural beauty is a source of terror, the sign of a latent savagery in Hérodiade, of fearful deeds which are her destiny. The offer of perfume is an attempt to adorn Hérodiade through the means commonly employed by women, and as a manuscript of the "Scène" with accompanying stage directions indicates,[36] the princess is infuriated at the mere suggestion. Free of any artificial contrivance, her hair will keep "*la froideur stérile du métal*," cruel, pale, and distant. The dominant function of the Nurse is to lead Hérodiade to a discovery and revelation of her inner self, by providing the most striking possible contrast of inner and outer realities. Yet, the tension exists not only between one character and another, but also within the central figure herself, for beauty so extreme both isolates and transforms. Just as the mirror provides the supreme evidence to Hérodiade of her uniqueness and individuality, it also reflects the emptiness that lies beneath her self-possession. The stage manuscript is brutally direct in utterance: "*Horreur, j'ai contemplé ma grande nudité!*" The action rises steadily in emotional intensity. The collision of opposing impulses, the sense of dread expectation, the unusual excitability and frenzy of the central character, the unconscious resistance of the Nurse, the presence of dark mysterious forces on the edge of events which neither character can ascertain, the suspense and wonder that hover over all—these are all part of an increasingly absorbing dramatic situation which we come to understand only to the extent that we grasp the intricacies of Hérodiade's character.

Above all else, Hérodiade is proud. Her mystery and her

splendor exist for herself alone; isolated from life, her sterility is a challenge to the physical fact of existence itself. Her joy in her self-possession is her supreme glory and fulfillment. Yet, this beauty, with no object other than that of self-contemplation, imposes its penalties of incompleteness and pain: "*pour qui*," the Nurse queries, "*dévorée/D'angoisses, gardez-vous la splendeur ignorée/Et le mystère vain de votre être?*" Consumed by passions she cannot satisfy, Hérodiade suggests the measure of her suffering only by the intensity of her assertions of inviolability. The Nurse, with her assurance that Hérodiade's pride will someday fall, drives the princess to a declaration of the meaning of her existence: she wills the cold terror of her virginity as the condition of consciousness itself. Her powerful declamatory statement, beginning with the lines, "*J'aime l'horreur d'être vierge et je veux/Vivre parmi l'effroi que me font mes cheveux*" is in fact a dialog between Hérodiade and her mirrored image—the self luxuriating in the contemplation of its image, yet aware of the isolation and anguish that this contemplation imposes. Robert de Montesquiou called Hérodiade "*une sorte de Narcisse feminin*";[37] she is perhaps the supreme expression of narcissism in modern literature, but a Narcissus intellectualized, tormented and maddened in the very moment of intoxication before the mirror, yet finding in this torment the fullest pleasure that life can hold. Cold, solitary, hard, a prisoner of her willed sterility, Hérodiade is eternally conscious of her awareness of this existence, as though she were saying in her most lucid moments of perception: in the mirror I see myself seeing myself.[38] We can readily understand why some readers have found in her drama the groundwork of Valéry's *La Jeune Parque*.[39] Yet, Hérodiade knows too that her dearly bought equilibrium cannot last. Her hatred of external beauty, of the realm of the imagination, of "*le bel azur*," is a final gesture of defiance of a world soon to overwhelm her, and her closing words, uttered to herself after the Nurse has left the scene: "*Vous mentez, ô fleur nue/De mes lèvres. J'attends une chose inconnue*" point to the impossibility of her continued defiance.

We cannot be altogether sure of how Mallarmé originally

planned to end his drama, for virtually all of our knowledge of the poet's projected conclusion dates from the latter part of his career. The testimony of a young contemporary is instructive. In Hérodiade's final lines, Robert de Montesquiou declared, "*elle ébauche le secret, lequel, je le tiens du poète lui-même, n'est autre que la future violation du mystère de son être par un regard de Jean qui va l'apercevoir, et payer de la mort ce seul sacrilège.*" [40] Nowhere does Mallarmé suggest the slightest physical contact; [41] in all likelihood, the "violation" of Hérodiade will be purely spiritual. Similarly, her tragedy does not reside in the violence she commits, which Mallarmé nowhere describes and which he could take for granted in the conduct of the action. Her tragedy lies rather in the total destruction of the temple of worship she has created and in which she dwells; in the subversion of her inviolability in which life exacts full payment from her who most spurns it. With her will broken, her existence is at an end.

The "Cantique de Saint Jean" is only loosely connected to the earlier parts of the poem. [42] In neither the "Ouverture" nor in the "Scène" is Saint Jean mentioned by name, nor is there the slightest allusion to Hérodiade in his "Cantique." Calm has replaced the dread expectations and feverish tensions of the earlier sections, and mystery has given way to certitude. Saint Jean dies exultantly aware of his salvation and transfiguration. [43] The earlier parts of the poem are suggested by the musical analogy, which resolves the preceding stress and strain by transferring the earthly scene of events to a higher plane of reality.

Even without the sections of the poem which enclose it, the "Scène" offers abundant proof of Mallarmé's skill and power as a dramatic poet. The economy of narrative, the swiftness of pace, the fluid interplay of foreshadowing and surprise, the atmosphere charged with suspense, the inevitable movement toward a climax, all belong to the art of drama. Fundamental to Mallarmé's dramatic technique is his skill in creating and revealing hidden dimensions of character. We learn more about Hérodiade in a few short lines than we might learn from hundreds of pages of fictional reportage. The interplay of conflict within and around the central character, the diametrical opposition of the heroine and the world of common experience, provides a drama of immense proportions. Isolated and introspective, Hérodiade may seem at first glance more contemplative than active, but her destiny is to do and to suffer, and the conditions of her free personal existence are bound to collide and fall before the events which lurk on the edge of the action. We see Hérodiade poised on the brink of catastrophe. Her destruction is implicit in the plot as well as in her character, and the initial dramatic scene offers full preparation for the tragic denouement.

Mallarmé's abandonment of *Hérodiade* as a play is understandable, but in view of the undeniable dramatic power of even the few scenes that we have, we may be permitted to share the reaction of the poet's friend, Aubanel, who declared in a letter to Mallarmé of November 1865: " Je regrette que pour ton *Hérodiade* tu abandonnes la forme dramatique, jamais le poème n'est aussi vivant que le drame." [44]   Mallarmé's abandonment of the dramatic form undoubtedly stems from his disillusionment with the stage following his visit to Paris in the early fall of 1865, but it may also rise out of a deeply-seated disdain for the theater of the day. In February of 1865, he had greeted with unusual enthusiasm Villiers' *Elën*, "*un drame en prose pour lequel le théâtre serait trop banal.*"[45] Clearly the young poet distinguished sharply between drama for the stage and for the study, and yet, following the example of Banville and Villiers, he believed genuinely in the possibility of a literary drama; the composition of *Hérodiade* was a deliberate act toward the realization of this ambition.

By July 1868, if not earlier, the "Scène" was entitled "*fragment d'une ancienne étude scénique d'Hérodiade*";[46] yet Mallarmé had not altogether abandoned it, and with the subsequent discovery by young admirers of his early work, especially after 1884, following the efforts of Verlaine and Huysmans,[47] the poem was forced on Mallarmé's attention. In 1886 he planned to complete *Hérodiade* and to publish it as a little book.[48] No doubt other literary and theatrical pursuits intervened, and the project was deferred. In the last two years of his life, the poet returned to the dramatic poem, which he saw as embracing five parts, and in the note on his literary heritage, penned shortly before his death, he alludes to "Hérodiade, *terminée s'il plaît au sort.*" The title of the finished work was to be *Les Noces d'Hérodiade. Mystère.* [49]

Now that the notes and drafts for Mallarmé's work have been published, thanks to the efforts of Gardner Davies, we can see that the composition of 1898 constituted a return, at least in part, to dramatic dialog and the physical demands of stage presentation. The new work apparently comprised a "Prélude," replacing the "Ouverture"; the "Scène" between Hérodiade and the Nurse; an intermediate scene culminating in the demand for Jean's head; "Le Cantique de Saint Jean"; a final "Monologue" setting forth the "*pourquoi de la crise*"; and a "Finale." [50] The movements are broken and disconnected; the dramatic action is climactic rather than consecutive, with one crisis rapidly following another. *Les Noces d'Hérodiade* offers only the outline of a drama, much closer conceptually to the vision of the theater which Mallarmé elaborated in the last decade of his life than to the Parnassian drama of the 1860's. Nevertheless, Mallarmé's *Mystère* offers the substance of effective theater as well as richly evocative poetry, and it is regrettable that it was unfinished.

The symbolic values of *Les Noces d'Hérodiade* are deep and complex. The wedding alluded to in the title represents "*le mariage du génie sans nom, porté à l'ultime degré de perfection, et de son rêve de beauté idéale.*" [51] The "meaning" of the work is abstract and conceptualized, far removed from the concrete interplay of character in action that we find in the "Scène" of 1865. Descriptive and anecdotal elements have given way completely to the inner drama of Mallarmé's "*jeune intellectuelle,*" [52] intimated or evoked in the movement of the poem. Dialog serves not to propel the action, but to reveal the significance of the monolog or inner drama. In one of his notes, Mallarmé schematized this internalization of dramatic elements: [53]

> pensé
> monologue —
> silence et danse —
> attitudes —
>
> seul monologue
> éclat intérieur

It is tempting to speculate on the role of the dance in the *Hérodiade* of 1898. In his "Préface," Mallarmé emphasizes the difference between his heroine and "*la Salomé je dirai moderne ou exhumée avec son fait-divers archaïque—la danse, etc.*" [54] Very probably, Mallarmé had Oscar Wilde's *Salomé* in mind, but his conception of Hérodiade as an imaginative rather than a historical figure, "*un être purement rêvé*," [55] goes back to the very beginnings of the work. A note for the later "Préface" emphasizes the internalization of physical movement: "*déplacement de la danse—ici—et pas anecdotique.*" [56] It may well be that the dance in *Les Noces d'Hérodiade* is pure metaphor, spiritual rather than physical movement.

We may see in the *Mystère* of 1898 the same detheatricalization that is characteristic of Mallarmé's symbolist dramatic theory. Linear anecdote is replaced by a wholly poetic evocation, not of the adventure of Hérodiade, but of its inner consequences, rarefied and abstracted through the poet's vision. The rejection of the conventional sources of dramatic effect is complete: [57]

> légende dépouillée
> de danse
> et meme de la
> grossièreté—
> de la tête
> sur le plat—

It is not likely that *Hérodiade* would have taken on traditional dramatic form had Mallarmé lived another ten—or hundred—years, and we cannot demand from it the qualities of a developed stage play. The drafts and fragments of *Les Noces d'Hérodiade* constitute poetry of a high order, some of which is among Mallarmé's very best; from this standpoint alone, it deserves to be studied and reread.

Even in its present form, the dramatic elements of Mallarmé's poem are considerable. Its unique values as well as its limitations rise in large part from the unusual character of Mallarmé's heroine, whose cold, metallic perfection is not intrinsically dramatic material, but whose collision with the world outside is fraught with the possibility of compelling dramatic action. Mallarmé's doctrine of effects forced him, even in the early stages of composition, to reject any literal presentation of events and to emphasize mood and suggestion rather than the overt antagonism of character in conflict. Clearly, this does not make for drama in the manner of Shakespeare or Victor Hugo, to say nothing of Sardou or Dumas fils, but it is a drama which Mallarmé's young admirers read and understood at the end of the nineteenth century.[58]

Even within the severely restricted limits of Mallarmé's composition, the "Scène" of *Hérodiade* is a remarkable fusion of seemingly disparate poetic and theatrical elements. Its poetic splendor is fully communicable in the theater.[59] The "Scène" has received at least three stage performances in Paris: one at the Théâtre Idéaliste on June 11, 1913;[60] another at the Théâtre de la Renaissance on November 14, 1919;[61] and still another at the Comédie Française in March 1937.[62] Without neglecting the purely literary qualities of Mallarmé's poem, we may say that the "Scène" almost cries out for stage presentation. Had he composed the rest of *Hérodiade* in this manner, Mallarmé would surely have produced a work that would hold and indeed enthrall an audience in the theater. We may well wonder if the change from "*tragédie*" to "*poème*" did not entail far greater loss than gain.

Hérodiade is not Mallarmé's "Grand Œuvre," even though it may have formed part of this ideal, at least in its early stages of contemplation;[63] but it is the work of a poet of prodigious talent. Remy de Gourmont called it "*le poème le plus pur, le plus transparent, de la langue française*,"[64] and his view has found many supporters. If Mallarmé had succeeded in reconciling in his art the conflicting claims of poetry and drama, he would have produced in *Hérodiade* one of the truly great achievements of European dramatic literature.

As it now stands, *Hérodiade* is best viewed as a lyric drama, an austere attempt to maintain the purity and dignity of the written word in the setting of a stage play. In this context its historical function and its intrinsic value come together. *Hérodiade* is Mallarmé's foremost achievement in the drama, rich and vibrant in its exploitation of the magic of poetry and more compelling still for the wonder of the universe it reveals. It is among the very first significant efforts toward a symbolist drama, and it is in such works as the plays of Villiers de l'Isle-Adam and Maurice Maeterlinck, the lyric dramas of Hugo von Hofmannsthal, and the poetic dramas of W. B. Yeats that Mallarmé's efforts were to find a degree of fulfillment in the modern theater.

Exhausted by the rigorous demands of his first efforts at dramatic composition, Mallarmé, in the early summer of 1865, turned away from the vision of cold, imperturbable beauty to take up "*un intermède héroïque, dont le héros est un Faune.*" [65] Readers of Mallarmé's " Églogue " may not easily recognize the theatrical elements inherent in its conception: " je le fais absolument scénique," the poet declared in his annunciatory letter, "non *possible au théâtre* mais *exigeant le théâtre.*" Nowhere else in Mallarmé's writings do we find so strong an expression of the will to drama. Undoubtedly the example and encouragement of Banville spurred the young poet to do all he could "*pour notre cause,*" the cause of poetic drama. Banville genuinely admired Mallarmé's "*vive et pénétrante poésie,*" and promised in a letter of late July 1865 to read and criticize both *Hérodiade* and the " Intermède." [66] Banville saw in his disciple a talented ally in his efforts to fuse poetry and drama in the theater; his cause, and Mallarmé's, was that embraced by all poets who would strive to recover their rightful place on the stage. Banville in 1865 was an experienced playwright, and it is not likely that he would have encouraged Mallarmé had he not considered him a promising dramatist. This ready offer of advice and help may have been responsible for the unusual energy and haste with which Mallarmé composed the "Intermède." It is almost with astonishment that Mallarmé declared to Lefébure in July of 1865, "Je suis, depuis une quinzaine et pour quelque temps encore, en pleine composition théâtrale." [67] The playlet which Mallarmé took to Paris in September may very well have been completed by the beginning of August: [68] a rapidity of composition unusual and perhaps unique for the poet. Mallarmé's animated description of his work on the *Faune* offers a sharp contrast indeed to his tortured labors on *Hérodiade*.

The poet's joy over the completion of his work was not to last. In September 1865, presumably at the Comédie Française, he read his "Intermède" before Banville and Constant Coquelin. The result, as Mallarmé reported to his friend Aubanel shortly after returning to Tournon, was disastrous: [69]

> Les vers de mon *Faune* ont plu infiniment, mais de Banville et Coquelin n'y ont pas rencontré l'anecdote nécessaire que demande le public, et m'ont affirmé que cela n'intéresserait que les poètes.

Mallarmé's discouragement is understandable, but he might have taken comfort from the apparently genuine praise of his critics for his verse. A subsequent letter of Emmanuel Des Essarts to Mallarmé suggests that Coquelin's rejection was by no means final. Des Essarts urged revision of the *Faune* for theatrical performance and added, "Coquelin croit que tu peux en tirer un excellent parti." [70] However, by May 1866, Mallarmé had altogether rejected any possibility of stage presentation of his poetic dramas of the preceding year and was in no mood to consider reworking them. His return to the *Faune* in the spring of 1866, again as relief from "*le cher supplice d'*Hérodiade," [71] was without the slightest concern for the demands of the theater. The revisions of 1866, in all likelihood, carried the poem a considerable distance toward "*L'Après-midi d'un Faune*."

The reader of the sections of Mallarmé's "Intermède"

which have been published may well wonder: what was the manuscript brought to Banville and Coquelin like? As in the case of *Hérodiade*, the relative inaccessibility of manuscripts and texts makes any judgment a matter of conjecture.[72] It seems reasonable to suppose that the work Mallarmé read in Paris was in three scenes rather than one.[73] Presumably, the "Intermède" opened with a monolog of the Faun, then moved to the "Dialogue des Nymphes," and concluded with a "Finale" that returned to monolog. The "Monologue d'un Faune" reprinted in the appendix to Mallarmé's *Œuvres complètes* (1450-53) is almost certainly not the text of August 1865, but a reworking, probably of 1866, although it could date from an even later period prior to 1876.[74] Mallarmé, in his letter to Lefébure of July 1865, alludes to a drama of close to 400 lines.[75] Even if we include the "Monologue d'un Faune" as part of the original version, we do not have more than half of the complete work.[76] Very probably, we have in fact a good deal less. In all likelihood, only the excerpts recently published in *Les Lettres* and *Empreintes* were part of the original manuscript.[77] Our knowledge of the text of the "Intermède" is deplorably incomplete at the present time.[78] In particular, a gap of perhaps 150 to 200 lines seems to exist between the "Dialogue des Nymphes" and the excerpt from the "Réveil du Faune." Mallarmé's correspondence suggests that the "Finale" of his "Intermède" must have been a scene of large sweep and high dramatic interest;[79] its discovery and publication would be a contribution of the highest order to our knowledge and appreciation of Mallarmé's art.

In spite of the complex textual difficulties obstructing any reconstruction of the "Intermède" of 1865, Mallarmé's comments on his work in his *Correspondance* enable us to draw certain conclusions. First and foremost, there can be no doubt of the theatrical character of the "Intermède": "Je compte porter cela à la *Comédie Française*," he declared to Lefébure.[80] Clearly, the poet envisaged his work as a stage play, not simply as a poem.

Secondly, but no less important, the language of the "Inter-

23

mède" represents a fusion of the idiom of poetry and drama. Mallarmé was vitally concerned not only with the theme and narrative, but also with sound and rhythm which he considered both poetic and dramatic in function. In the process of composing his drama, Mallarmé encountered the central problem which beset his master, Banville, and which has pursued a great number of playwrights in the past hundred years: how can the writer of poetic drama reconcile the conflicting claims of poetry and the theater? [81] In 1865 the attempt to fuse the two genres created difficulties for Mallarmé, but he was convinced that with effort they could be overcome.[82] On the one hand, the poet must create a line that is striking and original in its lyricism; on the other, he must enchant as well as inform the audience in the theater. Mallarmé believed that he had found "*un vers dramatique nouveau*" in which poetry and drama moved hand in hand. His "Intermède" would be compelling theater precisely because of the effectiveness of the poet's language and its interaction with gesture and dramatic action.[83]

As a poetic drama, the *Faune* must be viewed within the context of the revival of antique and mythological themes and forms in the French drama of the middle years of the nineteenth century.[84] In its legendary and traditional setting, "*toute parnassienne dans son paganisme décoratif*," [85] Mallarmé's interlude is an expression of the "*rêve hellénique*" that animated Leconte de Lisle, Banville, and their confreres. We have observed the preparation for the *Faune* in the early idyl, "*Loeda*," and there is no doubt that the origins of the poetic drama lie, at least in part, in Mallarmé's earlier work. Of primary importance, however, both in inspiring Mallarmé to create a poetic drama for an audience in the theater and in the precise formulation of detail in the "Intermède," is the role of Théodore de Banville. Mallarmé's *Faune* is a direct expression of the crisis of the literary drama in the 1860's as experienced and described by Banville, and there is no doubt that Mallarmé saw himself as a continuator of Banville's aspirations.[86]

This continuity of tradition may be seen most clearly in the marked resemblances of detail between Banville's *Diane au*

Bois and Mallarmé's *Faune*, not simply in decorative and atmospheric qualities or in elements of characterization, but in innumerable verbal echoes.[87] Mallarmé probably did not see the performance of *Diane au Bois* at the Odéon in October 1863, but he owned a copy of the play published in 1864,[88] and he must have read it with keen attention as a guide to his own efforts. It is significant that ten years later, in *La Dernière Mode* (819), Mallarmé singled out *Diane au Bois* as one of the very few important literary compositions of the modern theater.[89] In spite of recent tendencies to disparage Banville's work,[90] it may well be that without Banville's inspiration and example, Mallarmé would not have even thought of writing his "Intermède." This is not to say that Banville's Gniphon and Mallarmé's Faun are identical or even similar in their attitudes and dramatic function. If Mallarmé were inspired by Banville, it is also undeniable that in theme and implication he went well beyond anything Banville had written or was to write. On the other hand, Banville's *Diane au Bois* is important, not only in calling our attention to one of Mallarmé's primary sources, but also in enabling us to see how, in departing from his sources, Mallarmé asserted his originality.

The sources of Mallarmé's "Intermède" of 1865 are many and complex. It is not likely that Mallarmé's work owes anything to Aubanel's pastoral drama, *Lou Pastre*,[91] and it is difficult indeed to see even the slightest resemblance between Mallarmé's nymphs and those of Wagner's *Tannhäuser*.[92] Among the authentic sources of the *Faune* we may include Hugo's *Satyre*[93] and George Sand's *Lélia*.[94] To be sure, Hugo's faun lacks the psychological curiosity of Mallarmé's, but in his broad philosophical reflections, embracing all of space and time, and in his assumption of the role of poet, singing of man's glory to the music of Apollo's lyre, the Satyre points toward the hero of the "Intermède."

It is also probable that Mallarmé was influenced by the second part of Goethe's *Faust*.[95] Goethe, along with Shakespeare, represented for the young Mallarmé the very summit of dramatic achievement;[96] in his enthusiasm over Villiers' *Elën*, he exclaimed: "*La conception est aussi grandiose que l'eût rêvée Goethe*," and the context clearly indicates that Mallarmé is referring to Part II of *Faust*,[97] which he probably read in the translation of Blaze de Bury.[98] Faust's soliloquy in the "Classische Walpurgisnacht," in response to the appeal of the nymphs hidden near the banks of the Peneios, unquestionably points to Mallarmé's Faun, not only in incidental atmospheric details, but also in the very language in which Goethe's hero expresses his passionate desires and his awareness of the gap between dream and reality.[99]

There are convincing reasons for accepting Goethe's dramatic poem as one of the several sources of Mallarmé's conception, but this does not reduce the importance of the Parnassian tradition and notably the example of Banville for Mallarmé's *Faune*. It is one thing to see *Faust* II as part of Mallarmé's inspiration, and quite another to view his "Intermède" as a second "Classische Walpurgisnacht."[100] There is a broad parallel between Faust, in search of Helen, luxuriating in the mythical and legendary atmosphere of ancient Greece, and Mallarmé's Faun, but Faust's quest is altogether different in scale, embracing a range of experiences and values that are absent in Mallarmé's far more restricted drama. Apart from a line or two, the similarities between the works of Goethe and Mallarmé are general and tentative rather than detailed and pervasive.

We must still view Goethe among Mallarmé's authentic forerunners, particularly for his impact on the French poet's aspirations toward a vast dramatic synthesis. The preoccupation with cosmic destiny that we may see in many of the grandiose poems and poetic dramas of French writers of the preceding generation—in Lamartine, Hugo, Quinet, Musset, and George Sand, to name but a few—is a direct result of the profound impact of *Faust* in France.[101] From Goethe, as well as from Villiers de l'Isle-Adam, Mallarmé acquired the vision of a drama universal in scope, embracing the destiny of the individual and of humanity. Certainly Villiers too owed much to Goethe, and the tremendous enthusiasm of the young Mallarmé for *Elën* rises out of the grandeur of conception which led him to place Villiers beside the author of *Faust* II. It may well be that here in the combined influence of Goethe and Villiers, Mallarmé received his first impetus toward the creation of the Great Work, L'Œuvre, which was to receive explicit formulation in 1866. The broad symbolic conflicts and values which Mallarmé saw in his "Intermède" of 1865 issue out of this cosmic quest.

The sources, proximate and remote, of Mallarmé's *Faune* help us to situate the work as an expression of a variety of literary origins and dramatic traditions. Yet, in our fascination with the backgrounds of Mallarmé's composition, we should not forget that what the poet did with his sources—the originality and vitality of his artistic transformation of his materials—is far more important than are the sources themselves. Mallarmé's remarks on this subject, made rather late in life, stand as a perpetual admonition to his commentators:

> Le poëte puise en son Individualité, secrète et antérieure, plus que dans les circonstances même exaltant celle-ci, admirables, issues de loin ou simplement de dehors (876).

In our uncertainty over the text of Mallarmé's verse play of 1865, we must accept the "Monologue d'un Faune" only as an indication of the nature of the central figure in the dramatic setting. The Faun is impassioned by desire, seeking the nymphs who have fled from him and who are concealed in the nearby woods. In no way a clown or comic butt in the manner of Banville's Gniphon, Mallarmé's satyr is a creature torn by the pangs of physical desire, by the claims of dream and longing as opposed to the emptiness of ordinary experience.

This internal conflict is no abstract opposition of illusion and reality; the nymphs are made concrete through physical movement and scenic evocation, with the stage directions pointing to vivid action accompanying the soliloquy. We must see the nymphs as the height of the Faun's passionate existence, their touch constituting a moment of rapture beyond any he has ever known. The Faun, "*avide/D'ivresse,*" intoxicated by memory and by the promise of passion, has virtually been driven out of his mind.

The antecedent exposition emerges slowly. The Faun had surprised a group of nymphs bathing; he seized two of them, and as he attempted to carry them off, they made their escape. The distraught Faun sees the nymphs as cold, cruel, and hateful; yet they have become the center of his existence and he cannot free himself from them. The drama is the quest of the Faun for full actualization of being through the satisfaction of this intoxicating passion.

It is not merely visual beauty which haunts Mallarmé's hero in the first scene of the play, but rather the simultaneous nearness and remoteness of the consummation of desire. Even in thinking of other loves and in losing himself in sleep, the Faun cannot escape the haunting presence of the nymphs he has lost. The "*Adieu femmes!*" with which he stretches himself out to sleep is clearly no final farewell.

In the second scene, we move from the pursuer to the pursued. The nymphs Iane and Ianthe are nearby and have overheard the Faun's soliloquy. Iane too has been affected by the brief physical contact, and she is drawn to the Faun by the very warmth of his passion, even while she trembles before his presence. The "Scène" presenting the meditations of the nymphs amid the beauty of the woods may not be complete as we now have it, but in its atmospheric richness and invitation to reverie and dream, it invests the drama with the mood of lyrical ecstasy and the promise of love. Iane has felt the quivering of desire. She seizes the Faun's flute to discover if it also partakes of her torment and to learn "*pourquoi tout l'azur enivré me regarde!*" Ianthe, mindful of the danger which threatens Iane—the impending loss of virginity and the cruelty of love—urges flight from the Faun; but Iane, fully aware of the risk, insists on remaining.

The stage is now set for the central scene of the drama: the "Finale." We have only a fragment of Mallarmé's conclusion, but from his letters we may gauge something of its central importance to the poet. At the beginning of his work on the piece, he wrote to Cazalis, "*l'ideé de la dernière scène me fait sangloter";* [102] clearly, it was this scene that marked the climax of the drama and reconciled the conflicting aspirations and feelings of the nymph and the Faun.

Precisely how this climax was to occur we can only guess. The development of the first two scenes would seem to require a second confrontation of Iane and the Faun, in which their mutual involvement and passion are communicated, perhaps by Iane's return of the flute. This gesture would serve at once as a sign of his permanent impact on her and a renewed expression of her impact on him. Perhaps in this mutual recognition the Faun acquires the virginity of the nymph, and through his consciousness of an absolute and overwhelming purity, he undergoes a total spiritual transformation. The conclusion of the "Finale" we may see as a return to monolog in which the Faun comes to terms not only with his passion, but also with the contingency and mystery of existence. We have only the final eighteen lines of the Faun's "reawakening," but they suffice to make us regret all the more keenly the absence of the rest. The poetry is magnificent. Nowhere does Mallarmé's "Finale" suggest the slightest haste or awkwardness of composition. In their musicality and lyricism, these lines rival any of the poetry of the preceding months at Tournon.

In our imperfect knowledge of the "Finale," we cannot easily share in the pathos of the parting of Iane and the Faun, but in the closing lines we see that Iane's virginity and her tears, expressive of her love, serve to bring about a rebirth of the Faun through which he gains permanent possession of the ideal: a spiritual immortality expressed in the deep reflective harmony and inner peace of the closing lines: [103]

> Par les sables, calmez, faunes, avec des airs
> Le doux hennissement des aurores marines
> Elevant sur la vague humide les narines.
> Si mon jeune roseau parmi la Grèce plut,
> Vous encore, tritons illuminés, salut
> Des conques au quadrige effréné, de la brume
> Vainqueur, et secouant les perles et l'écume,

Prélude ruisselant, plages, dauphins, lever,
Je veux, dans la clarté transparente, innover
Une âme de cristal pur que jette la flute
Et je fuis immortel, vainqueur en cette lutte,
Les femmes qui pour charme ont aussi de beaux pleurs.
N'est-ce pas moi qui veux, seul, sans que tes douleurs
Me forcent, Idéal limpide?
                                        A la piscine
Des sources, à l'horreur lustrale qui fascine
L'azur, je vais déjà tremper l'être furtif
Qui de leur glace va renaître, primitif!

The self-transcendence and self-mastery reflected in these lines and the complete sense of the Faun's oneness with the universe mark the philosophical as well as the dramatic climax of the "Intermède." It is here that the symbolic values of Mallarmé's cosmic drama move beyond the pastoral theme and setting and beyond the private preoccupations of his hero. Commenting on his *Faune* to Lefébure as he neared the end of his labors of composition, Mallarmé declared: "Mon sujet est antique, et un symbole." [104] Clearly, Mallarmé is here alluding to the broadly symbolic character of his drama, in the manner of Goethe's *Faust*, but his statement also suggests a more concrete and literal symbolism in the dramatic action. Thus, the Faun may be viewed as an analog of the poet, or as a means for Mallarmé's exploration of the nature and consequences of the artist's calling. [105] The tormented longing of the Faun for the possession of beauty may well have been the longing of the poet as well. It is not necessary, however, to limit the symbolic values in this way, for we may see Mallarmé's hero not only as an incarnation of the artist, but also as a generic representation of man, both as a sensual and spiritual being, torn by the conflict of dream and actuality, and in this sense, universally symbolic.

The complex implications of the *Faune* go far beyond those of Banville's light and frivolous pastoral drama. "Ce poème," Mallarmé declared to Cazalis, "renferme une très haute et très belle idée." [106] Here again, Mallarmé insists on the transcendent and symbolic values imbedded in the dramatic action. This lofty and supremely beautiful idea has been described as the pure notion of ideal beauty, expressed through the contrast of *"la réminiscence incertaine d'un acte et l'évocation idéale que l'art parvient à en tirer."* [107] Once more, we may ask if the central meaning is not universal as well as particular. The loss of passion implicit in the final acquiescence of the Faun is at the same time a gain in the realization of the purity of ideal beauty. The love of the Faun for Iane is expressed through his consciousness of the permanent possession of beauty, by which he triumphs over the contingency of time and the distance separating the ideal from reality. The annihilation of this distance in the spiritual transformation of the Faun constitutes the expression, in the most literal sense, of *"une très haute et très belle idée."*

The deeper implications of Mallarmé's work, by no means apparent at first glance, point to the paradox inherent in the very notion of a work *"absolument scénique"* which is at the same time primarily internal and conceptual in movement.[108] The conflicts and values of Mallarmé's *Faune* cannot be readily apprehended through the dramatic action alone, and for this reason we must view the "Intermède" as a failure to overcome the opposition of poetry and the theater. From what we know of Mallarmé's conception of the piece, it could not be otherwise. Yet, the complete text might reveal a keener sense of theatrical values than Banville and Coquelin were willing to grant; even in its present form, the *Faune* is moving dramatic poetry, although inadequate as a poetic drama.

It is not easy to measure Mallarmé's achievement in the *Faune*. It is plain that his aspirations outran the very possibilities of his dramatic conception: an "intermède" of 400 lines cannot hope to stand comparison with such great philosophical dramas of Western literature as *Hamlet* or *Faust*. Yet, viewed in relation to the drama of its time, the early version of the *Faune* is far superior to anything we may find in Banville or in other contemporary pastoral interludes. Mallarmé's poetic idiom was not suited to the demands of a long and sustained

drama with multiple characters and intricate character relationships, but for a short play, it is fully adequate. It may be that
Banville and Coquelin judged the "Intermède" too harshly.
Banville's earlier insistence on "*l'intérêt dramatique*" was not
neglected, despite his strictures, but the *Faune* unquestionably
demands more attentiveness and imaginative sympathy than the
audiences of the day were prepared to give. It is a pity that the
play was not available to the producers of the Théâtre d'Art
or the Théâtre de l'Œuvre, for an audience familiar with
Mallarmé's complex poetic idiom might find the play moving
and absorbing on the stage as well as in the study.

The failure of Mallarmé at the Comédie Française entailed
more than the loss of what might have been a magnificent
poetic drama; it forced him to abandon not only his subject,
but the theater as well, and the resumption of *Hérodiade*, "*non
plus tragédie, mais poème*," testifies to his sense of defeat. In
retrospect, it would seem that the young poet yielded too easily.
His early dramatic attempts reveal far more insight into the
groundwork of motivation and the recesses of character in
action than one finds in many playwrights of the day who were
more successful than Mallarmé in plot construction and in
satisfying the demands of their public for short-run and easy
entertainment. Our view of Mallarmé as a poet should not
blind us to his real, if limited, dramatic talents. From a strictly
literary standpoint, the *Faune* of 1865 is bound to suffer when
compared to the poem of 1876; [109] the early composition should
be viewed in relation to the poet's dramatic and theatrical ends.
The *Faune*, with its sensual and concrete idiom, is remote indeed
from the purely poetic situation of "*L'Après-midi d'un Faune*,"
wherein the interpretation of the Faun's experience is "*de
plus en plus spiritualisée*." [110] Even in its unfinished state, the
Faune of 1865 is essentially different in its interplay of poetic
and dramatic values from any of Mallarmé's later poetry. There
is no need to disparage the one for the sake of the other; what
we have of Mallarmé's efforts in poetic drama suggests a more
considerable dramatic talent than almost any of his interpreters
have been willing to admit.[111]

It is significant that the poet himself, several years after his *échec* in the theater, was again attracted to the scenic possibilities of his subject. In November 1890, he wrote to his Belgian publisher, Deman, "On me propose de monter au théâtre l'Après-midi d'un Faune, qui est, en effet, écrit comme intermède scénique, à l'origine." [112] Mallarmé proposed a new edition of his poem, to include reflections on poetry and the theater, as well as "*le point de vue exact d'une mise en scène.*" Evidently, some of Mallarmé's admirers proposed a dramatic performance of "*L'Après-midi d'un Faune,*" perhaps for the Théâtre d'Art, to take place in 1891. In all likelihood, the poem was to be recited by a talented actor, who would perhaps combine mime and dance in his presentation. In this final version, the *Faune* would be simply "*un monologue en vers,*" closely resembling some of the dramatic odes of Banville. Mallarmé was quick to warm to the theatrical possibilities of the work: "*ma mise en scène, vivante, avec l'aide de quelques peintres, fera événement.*" In his collection of 1891, *Pages,* Mallarmé announced "*L'Après-Midi d'un Faune, edition nouvelle pour la lecture et pour la scène*"; [113] unfortunately, this project was without result. We do not know nearly as much as we could wish about the proposed dramatization of 1890-91, but it is significant that even at this distance from the original composition, Mallarmé was keenly aware of the theatrical values of his poem. These were to find larger expression in the celebrated Nijinsky ballet; yet there is more dramatic action in the early version of 1865 than we may see in the transposition of poem into dance. [114]

When we consider the *Faune* in relation to *Hérodiade,* the role of the "Intermède" as part of Mallarmé's early dramatic aspirations becomes clearer. *Hérodiade* was the poet's primary dramatic concern; the *Faune* was only a temporary interruption which came to acquire an importance of its own, but which never loomed as large in the poet's mind as the work which it momentarily displaced. [115] The difference is not only a matter of scale. The sensual and passion-driven Faun is directly opposed to Hérodiade and her refusal of physical experience, [116]

33

although the obsession with virginity of the princess may be an inverted assertion of passion, moving side by side with her insistence on the denial of the senses. Even in departing from *Hérodiade*, the *Faune* retains much of the Racinian idiom of the earlier "Scène." The probing self-analysis and sudden revelation of character of the *Faune* stem directly from the development of the poet's art in *Hérodiade*. Yet, while the evocation of mood is more sustained in the earlier piece, the language of the *Faune* is more immediately comprehensible; it is at once concrete and sensuous as well as vividly suggestive, marked by a poignant and arresting interplay of feeling and expression. Both works are inherently dramatic, and both may be viewed in retrospect as important experiments in the creation of a symbolist drama, a drama of suggestion rather than statement, of inner rather than external movement, of mystery and spirituality, directly opposed to the reproduction of literal reality. In his time, Mallarmé's dominant influence on the formation of a symbolist drama was to come through his critical writings and through his personal relationships with young writers, but in a larger perspective we can see his own dramatic compositions as efforts in the same direction. In their dramatic values and limitations they provide a striking demonstration of the complexity of the task confronting Mallarmé and his followers. It would be too easy to conclude from Mallarmé's failure that symbolist theories and techniques cannot find expression in the theater—a conclusion that is refuted not only by Mallarmé but also by Villiers de l'Isle-Adam, Maeterlinck, Hofmannsthal, Claudel, Strindberg, Yeats, and a host of other playwrights. It may well be that had Mallarmé come to the theater twenty-five years later he would have ranked among the major poetic dramatists of our time. His ability to combine the resources of poetry and drama may have found even more significant expression in a more favorable artistic climate. Even in their present unfinished state, *Hérodiade* and the *Faune* deserve high praise for their revelation of a new mode of dramatic composition. Without both the precept and example of Mallarmé, the redefinition of dramatic form provided by the symbolist playwrights could not have come about. The early dramatic attempts are compelling reading, for they partake of the same qualities which enhance all of Mallarmé's writing during his stay at Tournon; but they testify to a larger ambition—the conquest of the theater—which Mallarmé never abandoned, and which he achieved, perhaps better than he knew.

II

IGITUR AND HAMLET

IN SPITE OF THE KEEN DISAPPOINTMENT
that Mallarmé suffered in September of 1865, his attempts to
write for the stage were not altogether fruitless. In the years
immediately following, at a time when Mallarmé wrote relatively little, his theatrical interests and ambitions remained alive.
In his meditations on problems of aesthetics and particularly in
his formulation of "L'Œuvre" as the ideal and culmination of all
of his literary endeavor, we may see an artistic as well as a philosophical preoccupation that was to become of great importance
in the poet's later career. It was the influence of Villiers de l'Isle-
Adam, more than any other single force, that maintained Mallarmé's interest in the drama at a time when he turned away
with disgust from the theater of his day. We have seen evidence of the tremendous impact of *Elën* on Mallarmé. His
enthusiasm did not vanish quickly, for in May or June of 1865
he planned to write an essay on Villiers' play;[1] perhaps if his
own theatrical ambitions had not been so pressing, he would
have done so. The following year Villiers published *Morgane*
and sent a copy of the play to Mallarmé by way of Lefébure,
but "*par une suite de circonstances bizarres*" it reached the
poet only after a considerable delay.[2] Mallarmé was too absorbed in his philosophical pursuits to reply at once, and his
reaction was not nearly as impassioned as it had been to *Elën*;
nevertheless, in a letter to Villiers of September 1867, he praised
the drama warmly: "*ce magnifique développement* de vous *que*

J'ai relu vingt fois." [3] Mallarmé's dramatic inclinations were at an opposite pole from the violent and lavish spectacle of Villiers' romantic melodrama, but the integrity and high purpose of Villiers' view of his art served as a reminder to Mallarmé of the dignity and intrinsic richness of the dramatic form.[4] Villiers' absorption with the theater and the powerful, ever-increasing impact he had on Mallarmé at this time undoubtedly helped to keep alive in the poet the hope of significant dramatic creation.[5]

Wholly in keeping with the internal concentration of action of his earlier dramatic pieces and with the freedom from the restrictions of the physical stage that he asserted in the wake of his *échec*,[6] Mallarmé's next theatrical attempt was a fusion of drama and prose narrative: " *un conte*," he declared to Cazalis in November 1869, "*par lequel je veux terrasser le vieux monstre de l'Impuissance.*" [7] In August of 1870 he read his *" récit dramatique "* to Villiers and Catulle Mendès during their visit to Avignon.[8] Crestfallen over the cold reaction, especially Mendès', Mallarmé discarded his work, and it was not until 1925 that *Igitur* was published. The text, with Mallarmé's drafts, notes, and marginal comments, must have been reworked in the poet's later years; it should be viewed, at least in part, as an expression of the dramatic theory Mallarmé elaborated after 1886. We cannot be completely sure that the text as it now stands corresponds in every detail to the final disposition of the work,[9] and a reëxamination of Edmond Bonniot's edition in relation to Mallarmé's manuscripts is much to be desired. Even so, *Igitur* presents a relative completeness in movement that the earlier verse dramas lack, and its central importance in Mallarmé's work, from a philosophical as well as a literary standpoint, is beyond question.

Writing in 1923, before the publication of *Igitur*, Henri de Régnier declared: " J'ai plus d'une fois entendu Stéphane Mallarmé parler de ce drame philosophique qu'il avait conçu dans sa jeunesse et dont le héros s'appelait *Igitur d'Elbenon*." [10] There is further evidence, from Mallarmé's manuscript notes, of his conception or reorganization of the work in dramatic form

(442). With at least partial justification, Paul Claudel could claim of *Igitur*, " *c'est un drame, le plus beau, le plus émouvant, que le XIXᵉ siècle ait produit.*" [11] Claudel is referring primarily to the inner drama that constitutes the action, but his analysis is in theatrical rather than strictly poetic or narrative terms.

Mallarmé invited the interpretation of *Igitur* as a drama in his epigraph:

> Ce Conte s'adresse à l'Intelligence du lecteur qui met les choses en scène, elle-même (433).

Fully in keeping with the mature poet's symbolist theory of drama, the action is performed in the theater of the mind rather than on the boards of the physical stage; but the structure and theme of *Igitur* are direct expressions of the young Mallarmé's dramatic aspirations.

Igitur, like *Hérodiade* and the *Faune*, is a cosmic drama of immense philosophical proportions, drawn after *Hamlet*, *Faust*,[12] and plays of kindred scope and spirit such as Villiers' *Elën*. The hero's interrogation of the universe, which shapes the movement of *Igitur*, suggests that the image of Hamlet was uppermost in Mallarmé's mind. Even though the name of Shakespeare's hero is not expressed, " *la silhouette du prince danois se détache continuellement dans le filigrane du récit.*" [13] We need not see Mallarmé himself as Hamlet to recognize Igitur as intellectually akin to " *le seigneur latent qui ne peut devenir* " (300). As we shall see in his later dramatic criticism, the image of Hamlet was at the very center of the poet's definition of symbolist drama.

The " Argument " of *Igitur* which precedes the action is divided into four sections, according to the parts of the work (434). However, Dr. Bonniot, following the order of the manuscript, marked out five divisions, inserting the " Vie d'Igitur " as the third part of the piece (427). We may view this five-part division as corresponding in symmetry and movement to a five-act play, with each section drawing on and going beyond all that precede it.[14] The drama exists not only in the radical opposition of values, but also in the sequence as well as in the structure.

The first "scene"—a better term than "chapter" for the sections of *Igitur*—is the evocation of "*une présence de Minuit*" (435), a Midnight that is personified, given both intrinsic and physical significance as the crystallization of all time. Igitur's revelation of the meaning of this particular midnight occurs against a background that is somber, mysterious, and hostile. The vagueness of the décor is itself a source of terror and dread, a shadow "*finie et nulle*" suggestive of total absence and emptiness, of the darkness that will come when the candle illuminating the old magic book in which the hero reads will be extinguished.

The mood of fear and impending doom is accentuated in the second scene, but Mallarmé begins with an ironic stage direction: Igitur disappears going down the stairs "(*au lieu de descendre à cheval sur la rampe*)" (436). The descent is plainly no physical act, although Igitur's gesture is highly theatrical. His movement is a plunge into the abyss of consciousness and existence.[15] The very absence of visual details forces our attention on Igitur's preparation for his departure: his meditations, his sense of "*inquiétude*," and his fear of "*le hasard, cet antique ennemi qui me divisa en ténèbres et en temps crées*" (438). Igitur is painfully aware of the contingency of the self and its fragile opposition to his "*Ombre incrée et antérieure.*" The "*hantise du double*" or obsession with an other self is again an echo of *Hamlet*,[16] while the obliteration of physical existence is a portent of the door to the tomb and "*la substance du Néant*" (439).

The third section is only a "*schème*" or outline, but it is of central importance in the enlargement of the plane of action. Igitur's monolog in justification of his existence is, in fact, a dialog with his unseen but present ancestors. Overwhelmed by the past of his race, by his acute consciousness of the finite, and by the increasing pressure of emptiness and *ennui*, Igitur seeks to penetrate the mystery of life. The assertion of self, the consciousness of his incompleteness, the "*maladie d'idéalité*,"

39

all serve to define his self-projection beyond time, not only as an artist,[17] but also as a man. The climax of "Vie d'Igitur" is a magnificent expression of triumph over contingency and the horror of eternity.

The physical participation of the hero in the dramatic action reaches its fullest expression in Scene IV, "Le Coup de Dés," which Mallarmé describes in a marginal note as "Scène de Théâtre" (442). The climactic moment of the narrative brings us to the philosophical center of the piece: the discovery and revelation of the meaning of the universe. Without reducing Igitur's casting of the dice to autobiography or allegory, we may see in this gesture an effort to conquer "*le hasard*" in the name of the absolute which Igitur has become for himself.[18] The act is a prelude to his death, yet the throwing of the dice is no suicidal gesture,[19] but a heroic opposition of the Infinite to the Absurd implicit in chance, and which not only poetry but also life itself attempts to surmount. It is Igitur who closes the magic book and blows out the candle. The casting of the dice does not obliterate "*le Néant*," but neither does it reduce the *possibility* of the triumph of the will over "*le hasard*." In his demonstration of this possibility, Igitur maintains the purity of his race,[20] which he joins as its "*suprême incarnation*" (442).

The final section is a brief and sudden falling away from the climax. The denouement, like the scene which precedes it, is altogether theatrical,[21] marking not only the death of the hero but also the reëstablishment of order and calm. The dissolution of Igitur carries with it the sense of a final curtain and the resolution of all the tensions of the drama. The persistence, amid the dominance of death, of "*le château de la pureté*," points to the victory and glory of Igitur in his magnificent challenge of "*le Néant*," now "*parti*," removed from the plane of action. The drinking of the poison in the vial brings Igitur a death which is also life. Like many a hero of later symbolist drama, he dies into life: "*il boira exprès pour se retrouver*" (450). It may not even be a half-truth to speak of *Igitur* as a "catastrophe."[22] The dominance of a décor of "*une solitude désespérée*" throughout the drama rises from the antagonisms and contradictions of life itself,[23] which Igitur accepts and over which he inwardly triumphs. The opposition of the Absurd and the Infinite—of the will toward eternity on the one hand, and the will toward "*le Néant*" on the other [24]— places Mallarmé at the forefront of existentialist thought. The theater of action is perforce the theater of the mind, of the inner self, but viewed on this plane, *Igitur* is indeed a drama of cosmic proportion such as Mallarmé envisaged in his earlier attempts at writing for the stage. It is characteristic of the poet's efforts that his most complex expression of genuinely dramatic conflict should have virtually nothing to do with the physical theater.

Igitur is the assertion of a sharp if not decisive break with the demands of the theater; yet it was not without theatrical consequences. Villiers' Axël is a direct descendant of Igitur, not only in his character and situation, but also in his philosophical attitudes.[25] Furthermore, Mallarmé's later dramatic theories and conceptions are at times closely related to his "*récit dramatique.*" Virtually every line of Mallarmé's essay on Hamlet in *La Revue Indépendante* in November 1886 could be applied with equal force to Igitur. It has been suggested that *Igitur* constitutes "*la première esquisse de l'œuvre rêvée par Mallarmé pendant toute sa vie.*" [26] It would perhaps be more accurate to see in Mallarmé's later elaboration of *Igitur* an expression of his theory of ideal drama. His schematic outline of the elements of the *Mystère* and his consequent redefinition of dramatic performance were set forth on "*deux pages de notes d'une écriture postérieure*" attached to the manuscript of *Igitur* (428-29). These same notes, which seem to date from around 1895, are a part of Mallarmé's plans for his "Œuvre" as conceived late in life.[27] There is no evidence, however, to suggest that *Igitur*, at the time of its composition, was planned as a conscious effort toward the realization of the poet's dream. On the other hand, *Igitur* is as close as Mallarmé was to come in constructing a work fully in keeping with his later views of the ideal drama, and it is altogether fitting to speak of it in this context as constituting for the poet "*la révélation du théâtre*." [28]

It would thus be wholly incorrect to see in the composition of *Igitur* a total abandonment of the demands of stage performance, but it is clear that the attitude of the poet toward writing for the theater underwent a significant change as a result of his trials. The young Mallarmé's meager association with the theater in Paris was almost wholly the result of his friendship with Banville, and it was in large part as a writer of lyrical interludes or sketches in the manner of Banville's compositions that Mallarmé hoped to support himself and his family in the capital after his resolve to leave Avignon for Paris. Presumably some time in 1870 he approached Catulle Mendès for advice and was bluntly informed: "Les saynettes poétiques ne sont pas jouées." [29] The Parisian theater, completely dominated by followers of Scribe who excelled in trivial comedy or realistic social drama, had no place for poetry.

It is therefore easy to understand why Mallarmé in 1871 made a sharp distinction between poetic or literary drama, addressed to the initiate, and commercial drama, addressed to the mass theater-going public. In March of the same year he informed Cazalis that he hoped to make his way on the Parisian stage; he had accumulated notes and plans for a number of theatrical compositions and, even at that moment, he declared, "Je fais un drame . . . que je crois heureux: trois scènes, en prose gesticulante; mais c'est *très raide*." [30] Mallarmé's compromise with his ideals must have been painful, but at least the poet recognized the limitations of the theater in his time and tried to come to terms with them. The attempt was doomed from the start. Exhausted by "*la grande fatigue de tout le jour, causée par ce labeur dramatique*," [31] Mallarmé could not carry out his plan; he first interrupted his labors on the drama,[32] and then turned away from them altogether. Instead, he began work on a comic satire, "*un Vaudeville, discréditant aux yeux d'un Public attentif l'Art et la Science pour un nombre possible d'années*." [33] Neither of these projects of 1871 has come down to us, but it is possible that while the longer drama may have resembled Villiers' recently performed *La Révolte*, which Mallarmé praised highly,[34] the poet's "*petit drame, s'adaptant aux curiosités les plus variées d'une foule,*"[35] was in the spirit if not the language of the *saynettes* of Banville. Mallarmé's long-admired friend was helping him with his publishing projects at this time,[36] and Mallarmé may have been counting on Banville's aid in gaining access to the theater in Paris. The evident relish with which Mallarmé described his sly attempt to hoodwink the bourgeois makes one regret that the notes and drafts have apparently vanished. The poet's plans for an invasion of the popular theater preoccupied him for several years; they provide yet one more illustration of his deep and abiding interest in the drama.

It was a result of his journalistic enterprise, *La Dernière Mode*, late in 1874, that Mallarmé came to know the theater in Paris intimately. The "Chronique de Paris" which he penned for each issue, as well as the calendar of plays which he regularly compiled, brought him into direct touch with the theatrical world, not only of Sarah Bernhardt, but of the Vaudeville, the Cirque, and the Théâtre-Miniature. Even if we grant that Mallarmé did not see all the plays on which he commented, we know by his own admission that he saw a great many.[37] To be sure, *La Dernière Mode* cannot be viewed from the same standpoint as Mallarmé's later critical writing; at best, it is facile journalism, readable and informative, but seldom much more. Mallarmé did not overestimate his reading public. Nevertheless, it must not have been easy for him to review plays by Augier, Dumas fils, Zola, Sardou, Daudet, or operas by Meilhac and Halévy. From the very first issue, Mallarmé's awareness of the low estate of the Parisian stage is evident: "*un Théâtre! si rien ne vaut que nous y prenions intérêt*" (717). It is no surprise to discover Théodore de Banville virtually the only playwright of the day whom Mallarmé genuinely admired.[38] Within the limits of a drama of literal representation, Mallarmé could accord high praise to Zola and to contemporary playwrights of kindred spirit, but he could not accept their reduction of the scope of drama. The "Chroniques" in *La Dernière Mode* are interesting in themselves as an index to the theatrical season of

1874, but far more important is the poet's vision of an altogether different theater, expressed in the conviction that *"l'art dramatique de notre Temps, vaste, sublime, presque religieux, est à trouver"* (717).

Mallarmé's dramatic projects at this time are a renewed assertion of his desire for a truly cosmic drama. We have observed the role of *Hamlet, Faust,* and *Elën* in the shaping of the poet's ambition to create a drama of universal philosophical import. Shakespeare, particularly *Hamlet,* was the dominating force in Mallarmé's dreams and visions of theatrical composition. Late in life, in an essay of 1897 on *Macbeth,* he recalled *"des années quand l'influence shakespearienne, souverainement, dominait tout projet de jeunesse relatif au théâtre"* (346). The poet's admiration for Shakespeare began early. In 1860 he purchased an abridged edition of Shakespeare's works, which he studied—no doubt with special attention to *Hamlet*—by way of preparing for the examination for a teaching certificate.[39] As early as May 1862, he openly compared himself to the melancholy Dane, *"ridicule Hamlet qui ne peut se rendre compte de son affaissement."*[40] Earlier that year in his poem, *"Le Guignon,"* Mallarmé saw the modern *"poètes maudits"* as *"Ces Hamlet abreuvés de malaises badins"* (1411); from virtually the beginning of his career as a poet, the image of Hamlet merges with that of the poet's self.[41]

The vogue of Hamlet in France in the later nineteenth century, along with the attendant view of the dreamer as the hero *par excellence* and *Hamlet* as the supreme achievement in the world's dramatic literature, unquestionably finds expression in Mallarmé's writings, early and late.[42] Like most of his contemporaries, Mallarmé viewed *Hamlet* as an analysis of existence, a drama of the mind, largely divorced from the material demands of stage production. The easy identification of nineteenth-century poets with Shakespeare's hero did not pass unobserved. Emile Montégut, a critic whom Mallarmé came to admire greatly,[43] protested against the tendency of the day: *"nous avons fait un Hamlet à notre image."*[44] Contrary to many of the poets, Montégut saw the play as a pattern of inaction followed by action; but his view of the first three acts, "*remplis de réflexions, d'irrésolutions, de projets et de rêves, de plans ébauchés et abandonnés*," [45] accords completely with Mallarmé's conception of the play as a whole. The same attitude toward Hamlet as a universal symbol, a representative of "*l'homme moderne*," is reëchoed over a decade later in the pages of the *Revue des Deux Mondes* in an essay of Blaze de Bury which it is very possible that Mallarmé read. *Hamlet* for Blaze is the central work of modern literature: "Œuvre profonde, immense," *Hamlet* "resterait pour notre dialectique moderne ce que fut Aristote pour l'homme du moyen âge." [46]

Mallarmé's image of Hamlet is in part that of his time; yet his view is not mythic but highly personal. It may be that the poet's conception was shaped less by literary judgments than by the painting of Hamlet by Manet, drawn after the performance of Rouvière, and displayed by Mallarmé on the wall of his apartment.[47] Manet's Hamlet is young, timid, and on the brink of physical annihilation.[48] He is the visual counterpart of Igitur.

We have already pointed to the close resemblance between *Hamlet* and *Igitur*. For Mallarmé, *Hamlet* too "*s'adresse à l'Intelligence du lecteur qui met les choses en scène*"; and just as the play was completely removed from the physical theater, so the character of "*le subtil Hamlet*," the embodiment of the probing intellect (785), existed uniquely as a pure idea. The spiritualization of character went hand in hand with the reduction or elimination of the stage.

There can be no doubt of a close and direct relationship between *Igitur* and Mallarmé's projected Hamlet drama of 1876. Our principal informant of Mallarmé's plans is George Moore,[49] whose literary memoirs are not infallibly correct in matters of detail; but Moore's recollections of Mallarmé seem to be confirmed by other sources. In a brief note published in 1909,[50] Moore described his first meeting with the poet, presumably in late 1875 or early 1876.[51] Mallarmé proudly informed the brash young Irishman that he was working on a play, which Moore subsequently came to call "Hamlet and the wind." [52]

45

The "Souvenir" of 1909, not easily accessible, takes the form of an interview:

En combien d'actes est votre pièce, maître?
— En trois.
— Et combien de personnages?
— Deux: moi et le vent.
Interroger le maître sur son scénario, qui devait être du reste d'une grande simplicité, me semblait impoli. J'attendais ses paroles. . . .
Un jeune homme, le dernier de sa race, rêve dans son château délabré. De quoi rêve-t-il? De guerres, de duels, d'aventures dans les forêts lointaines: enfin . . . de la vie.
. . . Projets sur projets . . . , et il demande à ses ancêtres de lui enseigner le chemin. Mais c'est toujours le vent dans la vieille tour qui lui répond, qui cherche à lui répondre.
It is the genius of the french language that the wind in an old tower seems to be always trying to say—ou-i.
Et le jeune homme écoute le vent . . . sans jamais être sûr si c'est « oui » que le vent veut dire.[53]

Moore does not seem to be aware of the deft irony of Mallarmé's description. The poet's account of his plans for the production of his play is clearly tongue-in-cheek, although Moore presents it as wholly serious:

Bien des fois Mallarmé m'a parlé de sa pièce, et quand je lui demandais où il voudrait la faire représenter, dans quel théâtre, il parlait de voyager en caravane et de jouer son héros lui-même dans toutes les foires de France. Il s'exaltait à l'idée que le poète serait lui-même son saltimbanque.
La pièce ne fut jamais écrite (tout au plus prit-il quelques notes) mais il la rêvait si bien, debout, devant le poêle, que je m'en souviens encore, ainsi que de ses mollets rôtissants et de son si beau visage.[54]

Mallarmé's description is not wholly comic, for the notion of the poet as sole performer of his works finds expression elsewhere,

46

notably in "*Le Pitre châtié*," and in the plans for the publication of "*Le Livre*." Yet, the tone of Moore's account intimates that he viewed Mallarmé's ambition as altogether chimerical. The publication of *Igitur*, which Moore evidently did not know, suggests a close correspondence with the dramatic project of 1876. In *Avowals* Moore again refers to this drama "consisting of a single character: a young man, the last of a race, who lived in an old castle in which the wind howled, inciting the young man to go forth and rebuild the fortunes of his family. But the young man is uncertain whether the wind bids him stay or go forth. . . ."[55] There is no indication in any of Moore's memoirs of the resolution of the play; the emphasis is on the central figure's indecision which is itself apparently the principal dramatic "action."

The close resemblances in detail between *Igitur* and "Hamlet and the wind" strongly suggest that the projected drama of 1876 stemmed directly from Mallarmé's earlier composition.[56] This is not to say that the two are identical; yet, as we can see marked overtones of Hamlet in the indecision of Mallarmé's "young man, the last of a race," so we can also find unmistakable allusions to Shakespeare's play in *Igitur*, not only in the principal sections, but also in the notes and drafts which were not incorporated into the body of the work by Dr. Bonniot, and which were published by him as "Scolies." In Igitur's descent, "*allant jouer dans les tombeaux*," we may see a direct analog of the gravedigger scene in Hamlet (450). In 1865, in his unrestrained enthusiasm for Villiers' *Elën*, placing it alongside of *Hamlet* and *Faust*,[57] Mallarmé said of the concluding scenes, "*elles égalent la scène du cimetière d'Hamlet*."[58] The gravedigger scene was among Coquelin's most famous portrayals, and Mallarmé was probably familiar with his performance. For the poet's contemporaries as well, the feelings and attitudes of Hamlet in this macabre setting exerted a curious fascination.[59] In *Igitur* the parallel is not developed explicitly: the injunction of Igitur's mother is outside of and anterior to the dramatic movement, but in the light of the profound imaginative hold of Shakespeare's meditative prince over Mallarmé

47

both before and during the composition of *Igitur*, the allusions are expressive of a pervasive similarity.

On the other hand, it is not difficult to point to statements and gestures in *Igitur* which correspond to those of the projected drama described by George Moore. In Scene IV, under the marginal heading of "Scène de Théâtre, ancien Igitur," Mallarmé wrote: "*Ne sifflez pas aux vents, aux ombres*" (442); and this command of the hero is expanded in the "Scolies": "*Ne sifflez pas parce que j'ai dit l'inanité de votre folie!*" (451). As in "Hamlet and the wind," there are but two characters: the poet-hero and the wind, whose mysterious utterances remind Igitur of the claims and injunctions of his ancestors. Both works share a common derivation from *Hamlet*; both are preoccupied with the same conflict of dream and destiny that Mallarmé was to describe, apropos of Shakespeare's play, as the only subject of drama (300). This is not to suggest that *Igitur* and "Hamlet and the wind" are identical. With all due allowance made for playful irony in the poet's description to George Moore, it is likely that the projected drama of 1876 is a direct development of *Igitur*, fused with elements of the popular theater which the poet derived from his journalistic pursuits of 1874.

In any case, it is difficult to see either *Igitur* or "Hamlet and the wind" as a popular melodrama, in the manner of the "vaudeville" of 1871. The melodramatic interest was reflected in other ways. Despite the poet's passion for Shakespeare and his lifelong admiration for Banville, he was well aware of the love of the masses for bold and striking scenic effects, and he seems to have taken genuine delight in the appeal of stage performance to an unlettered public. Early in 1876 he informed Arthur O'Shaughnessy, "Pour le moment, je suis en train de fabriquer le scénario d'un très gros mélodrame populaire, et ne lâche pas mon travail d'une minute"; [60] again, in March of that year, he declared to the same correspondent: "Je travaille à un vaste mélodrame populaire qui me prend jusqu'au sommeil et cela pour plusieurs mois de la vie interrompue que je mène." [61] It has been suggested that this work was the same

which Mallarmé described to George Moore,[62] but there is no
evidence in support of this conjecture. We have seen the poet
at work on two plays at the same time on more than one occasion, and it is likely that in 1876 a number of dramatic projects
were present in his mind. He wrote to O'Shaughnessy of a
decisive turning point in his career: "Il est probable que je ne
vais plus que faire des drames pendant plusieurs années." [63] His
theatrical ambitions were more alive than ever, and it is reasonable to suppose that Mallarmé did a great deal of work on the
popular melodrama to which he so repeatedly alluded.

It is tempting to see Mallarmé's later ritualistic theory of
the drama, which he came to elaborate in large part in response
to the appeal of Richard Wagner's vision of the art work of
the future, as already present in the dramatic aspirations of
1876. As we shall see, by this date Mallarmé knew something
about Wagner's art, but it is improbable that his theatrical
conceptions at this time owe anything to the German composer.[64] There is unquestionably a striking similarity in their
attitudes toward the fashionable theater of the day and their
desire to create a new dramatic form, but in 1876, the notion of
theater as a mass secular rite had only begun to take form in
Mallarmé's mind. It would be difficult to describe with any
certainty the technical qualities of the theater which the poet
envisaged; it was not, at this time, a poetic theater. In the
review "*Erechtheus*: Tragédie par Swinburne," which Mallarmé wrote in January 1876, he praises the English drama
uniquely from a literary standpoint (702). His own dramatic
ambitions were now clearly of another stamp, crudely theatrical
and lavish in the interplay of all the arts of dramatic performance.

Mallarmé's correspondence of the following year shows
how fervently he pursued his task of seeking to revolutionize
the modern drama. In a letter to Sarah Whitman, who had
been the fiancée of Poe, Mallarmé apologized for the delay in
the appearance of his translation of Poe's poems, pointing to his
dramatic preoccupations as the principal cause.[65] On January
12, 1877, he informed his American correspondent: "Ma
traduction est fort retardée (sa publication, du moins) par un

49

grand travail—un drame à faire jouer à époque fixe—qui joint à une vie trop affairée, me surmène et me brise. . . ." It would be interesting to know if Mallarmé's efforts at this time were accompanied by negotiations for production. A letter to Mrs. Whitman of May 28, 1877 tells us a good deal more about the poet's vast dramatic project:

> . . . Vous voulez bien me demander où en est mon travail dramatique; il avance, quant à moi, du moins; mais la grande tentative d'un théâtre entièrement nouveau à laquelle je m'adonne, me prendra plusieurs années, avant de montrer aucun résultat extérieur. Trop ambitieux, ce n'est pas à un genre que je touche, c'est à tous ceux que comporte selon moi la scène: drame magique, populaire et lyrique; et ce n'est que l'œuvre triple terminée, que je la donnerai presque simultanément; mettant comme un Néron le feu à trois coins de Paris. Il y a là un monde d'efforts, mental et matériel; et ma pauvre traduction de Poe en souffre. . . .

The description is still vague and general, but it is clear that Mallarmé has meditated deeply on the theoretical foundations of "*un théâtre entièrement nouveau.*" The simultaneous fusion of all of the dramatic genres suggests a grandeur and complexity of conception rivaled only by the Wagnerian ideal of total art, which it in some ways resembles. The immense time and energy which Mallarmé sees as necessary to the completion of his enterprise, and the gigantic effects which he envisions as its consequence, all point to the likelihood that the "*travail dramatique*" of 1877 is intimately associated with the poet's ideal of "L'Œuvre," or at least with one phase of its expression. In the summer of that year his efforts continued unabated, for he wrote to Mrs. Whitman on July 31: "L'ardeur avec laquelle je travaille à toute une vaste entreprise dramatique, un théâtre absolument neuf, cela au milieu des embarras de toute sorte . . . ." We have additional confirmation of his efforts with more precision of detail, in a letter written to O'Shaughnessy late in December of 1877:

Je travaille follement et j'étudie partout les fragments d'un théâtre nouveau qui se prépare en France et que je prépare de mon côté; quelque chose qui éblouira le peuple souverain comme ne le fut jamais empereur de Rome ou prince d'Asie. Tel est le but: c'est roide. Il faut du temps. Vous rappelez-vous Léona Dare (aux Folies-Bergère). Elle a sa place dans ce vaste spectacle.[66]

Once again, we see Mallarmé fascinated by the impact of performance on the mass public and by the demands of audience collaboration that the theater imposes.

The vast dramatic enterprise that would bring together all the arts and resources of the theater, including the music hall dance, assuredly has little resemblance to "Hamlet and the wind" or to any of Mallarmé's earlier ventures in dramatic composition. Perhaps the theory of drama set forth in the later 1880's in *La Revue Indépendante* and expanded in the critical essays of the 1890's is the fruit of a much earlier vision of a new theater. It would be of keen interest in our study of Mallarmé's contribution to dramatic theory and practice in the later nineteenth century, if the scenario of his multiple panoramic drama of 1877 had been preserved. Mallarmé's impact on the theater of his time was to grow along with his personal influence and the influence of his poetry, early and late, in shaping the new literature of the day, but the efforts of 1876 and 1877 are significant not only for the new vision of the theater which they reveal, but also because they represent the poet's last sustained attempt at dramatic composition. The vastness of Mallarmé's ambition was bound to intensify his earlier separation of the poet from the theater. While previously Mallarmé had tried to come to terms with the demands of the theater, now he wrote out of the conviction of the need for a totally new kind of dramatic performance, founded on an altogether different view of the art of drama from that of the realistic and representational stage. It is this experimental and revolutionary dramaturgy that Mallarmé was to incorporate into his symbolist aesthetic, which came to constitute the triumph of the poet in the theater.

III

HOMAGE TO WAGNER

MALLARMÉ'S VISION OF THE POSSIBILITIES of the drama is the counterpart of his lifelong aspiration toward an ideal art work, "L'Œuvre." This ideal was to receive a variety of formulations during Mallarmé's career, and it would be vain to try to identify it exclusively with any particular work. It is a dynamic, not a static concept, taking on new characteristics as the poet's experience came to be enlarged and his values defined or clarified. As the center and indeed the apex of Mallarmé's creative endeavor, "L'Œuvre" is one of the great unifying themes of the poet's mind and art: it haunted the meditations of the youthful poet just as constantly as it was to absorb him in later life, and no serious interpretation of his thought and expression can overlook its crucial importance.

The concept of "L'Œuvre" clearly underlies Mallarmé's vast dramatic projects of the 1860's and 1870's. Nevertheless, it is curious indeed, in the light of subsequent developments, that the poet's first allusion to this ideal has absolutely nothing to do with his dramatic aspirations. In a letter to Aubanel of July 16, 1866, Mallarmé declared: "J'ai jeté les fondements d'un œuvre magnifique."[1] His description is that of an ecstatic visionary, who sees the great poem as the consequence of spiritual resurrection. Mallarmé envisaged twenty years of labor before his work would be completed, but his rapturous account contains no hint of precisely what form this magnificent revelation of the mystery of existence would take. We cannot blame

Aubanel for his bewilderment in the face of Mallarmé's mystical outpourings,[2] the consequence, in part, of his reading and meditation on philosophical questions during the spring and summer of 1866. Three weeks after the poet's first allusion, he clarified his ideas for Aubanel's benefit:

> Je souffre beaucoup depuis quelque temps et d'une façon inquiétante—pour ceux qui m'aiment et surtout pour mon Œuvre, que j'esquisse entièrement en ce moment et qui peut être magnifique si je vis. Je parle de « l'ensemble de travaux littéraires qui composent l'existence poétique d'un Rêveur » et qu'on appelle, enfin, son œuvre. Es-tu éclairé, cette fois, cher ami? [3]

Clearly, at the very beginning, L'Œuvre was not a single grandiose work at all, but the totality of the artist's creative work. It is plainly incorrect to view *Hérodiade* as the first stage in the conception of L'Œuvre,[4] even if there is perhaps an adumbration in Mallarmé's earlier reference to the drama as "*un Rêve qui ne verra peut-être jamais son accomplissement.*"[5] More significant is the absence, in the poet's elaborations of L'Œuvre in 1867, of any mention of his dramatic projects. The notion of L'Œuvre underwent considerable change in 1866-67 [6] at a time when Mallarmé had turned away from the theater in disgust to rework his early dramas as poems, with the result that the dramatic elements were subdued if not altogether eliminated.

Thus, in the delimitation of L'Œuvre which Mallarmé set forth in his letter to Cazalis of May 14, 1867, he planned the ensemble of his composition as three poems in verse, "*dont* Hérodiade *est l'Ouverture,*" and four poems in prose.[7] The poet's preoccupation with philosophical premises and with L'Œuvre as a vast cosmic synthesis has led many of his interpreters to ascribe this ideal to the influence of Hegel.[8] It is likely that Mallarmé read Hegel, possibly in the summer of 1866,[9] and absorbed Hegelian terms and concepts into his aesthetic thought; but it is difficult to see the German philosopher in a role of central importance in Mallarmé's art. The ultimate source of Mallarmé's L'Œuvre may well be the poet's youthful dream

53

of a grandiose philosophical drama fusing *Hamlet* and *Faust*, and immediately inspired by Villiers' *Elën*, "*l'histoire éternelle de l'Homme et de la Femme*." [10] The origins of Mallarmé's aesthetic ideal are bound to remain a matter of conjecture and dispute, and they do not concern us here, but we may hazard the suggestion, in passing, that the ideological premises of L'Œuvre are to be found primarily in occult and mystical thought rather than in the Hegelian dialectic. Through Balzac, Baudelaire, Villiers de l'Isle-Adam, and a number of other writers, Mallarmé came into intimate contact with the magical and occult currents of the late eighteenth and early nineteenth centuries, which he assimilated as readily as Baudelaire had done before him, and which he came to express in his poetry as well as in his poetics. In his allegedly Hegelian letter to Cazalis, he closes with an invocation of "*mon œuvre, qui est L'Œuvre, le Grand' Œuvre, comme disaient les alchimistes, nos ancêtres.*" [11] Mallarmé's ideal is essentially part of a pervasive tradition in mystical speculation, and it should be reappraised in this context.[12]

The evolution of Mallarmé's aesthetic thought must be viewed as an expression of his artistic aspirations and of the literary and artistic currents of his time. It was evidently in the early 1870's, in the midst of his varied dramatic projects, that Mallarmé came to see his great art work as comprising elements of the drama.[13] It is possible to consider *Igitur* as part of this enterprise, not as a first draft of L'Œuvre,[14] but perhaps as a preparatory exercise in its composition,[15] for it is clear that *Igitur* issues from the same philosophical preoccupations that we have found present in the formulation of L'Œuvre in 1867.[16] Mallarmé's ideal was never abandoned, only changed, and the most significant modifications were made in the years following 1885, in response to the impact of Richard Wagner.

The influence of Wagner on Mallarmé is of capital importance in the development of the poet's mature dramatic theory.[17] The nature and degree of the impact of the German composer on Mallarmé have not always been clearly understood, largely because Wagner cannot be isolated completely

54

from other forces shaping the poet's thought and expression. Arthur Symons declared in his influential book, *The Symbolist Movement in Literature*: "Carry the theories of Mallarmé to a practical conclusion, multiply his powers in a direct ratio, and you have Wagner. It is his failure not to be Wagner." [18] It was Symons' failure not to have read Mallarmé more carefully. The differences between Mallarmé and Wagner are at least as striking and as important as their similarities. If, on the one hand, it in incorrect to see Mallarmé merely as the literary counterpart of the composer, it is also wrong to disparage Wagner's role and to hold it of little or no account in Mallarmé's later work. The relationship is complicated, and it deserves close examination.

The young Mallarmé's enthusiasm for Baudelaire in 1861 and 1862 may well have led him to the early discovery of Wagner. In the young poet's bold proclamation of the integrity and sanctity of art, "*Hérésies Artistiques: L'Art pour Tous*," written in 1862, Wagner is singled out as one of the keepers of the purity and mystery of art (257). Mallarmé's essay is markedly Baudelairean in inspiration and tone, and it is very probable that his awareness of Wagner is a direct result of Baudelaire's essay of the preceding year.[19] We cannot be sure, however, that Wagner was much more than a name to Mallarmé at this point, and there are no other allusions in the poet's early writings.

There is certainly no evidence of an awareness of Wagner's dramatic theories or techniques in Mallarmé's dramatic attempts of 1865. Both *Hérodiade* and the *Faune* "Intermède" are close to the poetic tradition of French classical drama and its reinterpretation in the middle years of the nineteenth century by Banville and others who sought to bring poetry and the theater into nearer accord. Even in later life, under the direct impact of Wagner, Mallarmé could contrast the operatic values and techniques which Wagner's disciples sought to adapt to the drama with those of Banville and other poets in the theater. Wagner was to enlarge Mallarmé's awareness of the possibilities of theatrical representation, but there is no sign of any

55

consciousness of these possibilities in Mallarmé's early attempts at the art of drama.

The revelation of Wagner's significance, not only for music, but also for all of the arts, came to Mallarmé in 1869 and 1870. In February of 1869 Baudelaire's critical essays were published under the title of *L'Art Romantique*,[20] and we may assume that Mallarmé read the critical writings as avidly as he had *Les Fleurs du Mal*. It is altogether possible that Baudelaire, who initiated Mallarmé into the writings of Poe, fulfilled the same role for Wagner. There were other ways too through which Mallarmé could have gained some awareness of Wagner's theories and art. In the *Revue des Deux Mondes* for April 15, 1869, there appeared a substantial essay by Eduard Schuré, "*Le Drame Musical et l'œuvre de Richard Wagner.*" We know that Mallarmé read the *Revue des Deux Mondes* in May 1867;[21] there is no reason to suppose that he was not still a reader of the leading literary journal of the day two years later. Schuré was to play a major role in the diffusion of Wagner's aesthetic thought in France in the later nineteenth century,[22] and it is possible that he may have been one of the principal intermediaries between Wagner and Mallarmé.

More important still was the role of Villiers de l'Isle-Adam.[23] Villiers' discovery of Wagner coincides with that of Baudelaire and may be a direct result of his warm admiration for the poet of *Les Fleurs du Mal*.[24] His wild enthusiasm for the German composer could have been communicated to Mallarmé in conversation, or in letters which we do not possess. In 1869 and again in 1870, Villiers visited Wagner, of whom he wrote with passionate fervor.[25] Directly following his second visit, in August 1870, in the company of Catulle Mendès and Judith Gautier, Villiers journeyed to Avignon and visited Mallarmé. In June, Villiers had dedicated his poem in prose, *Azrael*, "*A Richard Wagner, au prince de la profonde musique,*"[26] and there is no reason to suppose that the intoxication had worn off by the time of the visit to Avignon. Mendès had already informed Mallarmé of the pleasure which lay in store for him: "je me fais une fête de vous initier à l'art nouveau qui n'est ni la poésie ni la musique et qui est en même temps la musique et la poésie, crée par Richard Wagner." [27] Yet, it is doubtful that the visit of 1870 constituted Mallarmé's initiation, for in his impassioned essay of 1862, he had already referred to Wagner in language close indeed to Mendès' appellation of " *le précurseur et le rédempteur à la fois.*" Nevertheless, the correspondence and the visit which followed must be viewed as strengthening Mallarmé's recognition of Wagner's spiritual kinship, even if he was not moved at once to any new expression of admiration.

There are no indications of any deep familiarity on Mallarmé's part with Wagner in the early 1870's, either in his artistic thought or in his dramatic projects; but in a letter of July 1872, in which Mallarmé alludes to John Payne as " *un des nôtres,*" he goes on to state: " Il connaît la littérature française mieux qu'aucun d'ici, et adore et vénère Wagner." [28] Clearly, Mallarmé's attitudes were shaped by his contemporaries, and even if Villiers and Mendès did not necessarily enlarge his knowledge of the composer's works, they helped to create sympathy and receptivity for them. In a letter of 1876 Mallarmé alludes to an impending journey of Mendès to Bayreuth,[29] " *pour entendre la trilogie de Wagner.*" It is reasonable to suppose that from Mendès and other sources, Mallarmé acquired some notion of the " *Bühnenfestspiel*" without having made the pilgrimage to Germany.

Well before 1885, Mallarmé was aware of the cardinal elements of Wagner's aesthetic thought. Baudelaire's essay in *L'Art Romantique* alone would have served to provide more than a superficial introduction, for Baudelaire had quoted liberally from Wagner's " *Lettre sur la Musique* " of 1861. Despite his German wife, Mallarmé knew little or no German,[30] but Wagner's essay, written for the benefit of French admirers, incorporated many of the composer's leading ideas. Baudelaire called special attention to Wagner's view of dramatic art as a synthesis of the arts, which Baudelaire readily assimilated into his doctrine of *correspondances*. Mallarmé shared Wagner's essentially religious view of the artist's calling, and in Baude-

57

laire's essay could be found the same invocation of Greek ritual and of the theater as a temple and sacred shrine that Mallarmé himself was to assert in later life.[31] Wagner too had drawn upon the *Mystères* of the medieval liturgical drama in creating his panoramic vision of legendary and supernatural action. The internalization of movement along with the reliance on dream and atmospheric evocation—on a language of suggestiveness as opposed to statement—all received elaborate description and illustration in Baudelaire's rhapsodic account.[32] It is entirely possible that Mallarmé's reformulation of L'Œuvre in the 1870's owes something to Wagner's dramaturgy. Mallarmé's desire for a complex fusion of theatrical forms in a multiple and universally symbolic dramatic composition, such as we have seen expressed in the letters of 1877, may be a direct expression of Wagner's growing importance for the poet.

We should not forget that Wagner was not the only source of Mallarmé's dramatic theory and aspirations at this time. The ideal of a fusion of the arts in the theater and notably of an integration of poetry with all the physical elements of dramatic representation was a constant preoccupation of Théodore de Banville, whose essentially literary approach to the theater is at sharp variance with that of Wagner. Nevertheless, Wagner was to exercise a far more powerful hold on the poets of 1885 than he had a generation earlier. If Mallarmé's reservations were those of his elders, his genuine enthusiasm for Wagner was very much a part of the newer impulses animating the changing literary scene of the 1880's.

The popularization of Wagner in France was given tremendous impetus by the eulogies following his death in 1883, and by the steady flow of publications proclaiming the importance of his work.[33] The young disciples of Baudelaire and admirers of Villiers, Verlaine, and Mallarmé who called themselves "Symbolistes" saw Wagner among their authentic precursors. It may be somewhat of an overstatement to call the composer "the uncontested master of the French symbolist movement,"[34] but there is no question that he was one of the masters: "*sa conception de l'art, sa philosophie, sa formule*

même étaient à l'origine du symbolisme."[35] The organization
of the *Revue Wagnérienne* in 1884, under the aegis of Edouard
Dujardin, and with Villiers and Mallarmé among the announced
contributors, provided a rallying point for many of the young
poets of the day who saw a close similarity and even a virtual
identity between the Wagnerian aesthetic and the new awareness of suggestiveness and spirituality in poetry.[36]

The *Revue Wagnérienne* began publication in February
1885 and continued through July 1888. Its contents provide a
revealing illustration of the passionate but uncritical character
of much of the admiration for Wagner in France. Few of his
young enthusiasts had any direct familiarity with Wagner's
writings, and while the "*Lettre sur la Musique*" was of some
value as a statement of Wagner's vision of the art work of the
future, it was still only a pale and fragmentary version of the
great theoretical essays that were unavailable in French translation. Apart from the contributions of Houston Stewart Chamberlain and a small number of others, few of the discussions of
Wagner's art could be considered authoritative. All the same,
the *Revue Wagnérienne* is of real importance for its illumination
of the aims and values of the French writers themselves, who
used Wagner as a mirror and image of their own theories and
aspirations. The *Revue Wagnérienne* is one of the most valuable commentaries that we have on the doctrines and objectives
of the young symbolists. Wyzewa, Dujardin, and their confreres may not have always translated or interpreted Wagner
accurately; yet their efforts in the diffusion of Wagner's works
were to yield significant results in the development of the
theory and technique of both symbolist poetry and symbolist
drama.

Mallarmé conceived of his essay for the *Revue Wagnérienne*, "*Richard Wagner: Rêverie d'un poète français*," as
"*moitié article, moitié poëme en prose.*"[37] We should not read
it with the same expectations that we may bring to a rigorous
and systematic critical discussion. The density and complexity
of Mallarmé's style is itself part of the "*Rêverie.*" The poet's
use of language is fully in keeping with the definition of poetry

59

communicated to Léo d'Orfer in the preceding year: "La Poésie est l'expression, par le langage humain ramené à son rhythme essentiel, du sens mystérieux des aspects de l'existence. . . ."[38] The ellipses and syntactical inversions, the allusions, faint suggestions, and half-completed phrases, all characteristic of the poet's later critical writing, remind us that the dreamlike meditation on Wagner is itself poetry, even while it sets forth an attitude toward its subject that, for all of Mallarmé's vagueness and privacy, is nonetheless clearly defined.

The "*Rêverie*" must be read as an act of homage to a genius whom the poet greatly admired. We have already seen evidence of Mallarmé's response to the enthusiasm of Baudelaire and Villiers. His desire, as expressed to Dujardin, to write "*quelque chose d'original et de juste et qui ne soit pas à côté,*" indicates that he appreciated the importance of the *Revue Wagnérienne* and felt sympathetic toward its cause. The essay on Wagner is an occasional composition, the result in large part of Dujardin's importunate demands; but Mallarmé would not have writen it had he not felt deeply involved in Wagner's work and its implications.

The "*Rêverie*" thus constitutes an expression of sincere praise as well as of deeply-rooted reservations. Both attitudes are insistent throughout the essay. Mallarmé is fully aware that Wagner attempted to transform the old theater, and the poet has "*un regard affirmatif et pur*" for the composer's vision of the theater as it might become. It is this Wagnerian ideal rather than Mallarmé's Œuvre which constitutes "*le Monstre-Qui-ne-peut-Etre!*" (541). The description of Wagner's ideal art work is set forth in religious and ritualistic terms: the theater is to become a temple and the spectacle a ceremony in which the masses participate in a sacred rite. The totality of the drama "*ressent la colossale approche d'une Initiation.*" Here and throughout the "*Rêverie*," Mallarmé is passionately concerned with the impact of the new art form on the audience, and the reordering of the relationship between the stage and the mass public.

The grandiose reorganization of the arts of the theater

demanded by the composer is for Mallarmé a source of both astonishment and admiration. Not only "*l'apport de la Musique au Théâtre*" but the "*concours de tous les arts*" have brought about a total transformation of the stage, "*le miracle, autrement inerte et nul, de la scène!*" (542). In contrast to the old theater of literal representation, Wagner has created a theater of "*sortilège,*" of enchantment and magic, through the exploitation of all the arts of the theater, especially music, "*cette ressource nouvelle d'évocation.*" This theater, relying on suggestion, mystery, and vagueness as well as on a complex fusion of colors and sounds, themes, and movements, has acquired a new emotional intensity and a deeper spirituality than could ever be attained through simpler and more objective means. There is no doubt that Mallarmé appreciated the tremendous gain in breadth and depth of expression which resulted from Wagner's preoccupation with the interrelations of the arts in the theater.

Mallarmé's reservations in his view of Wagner's dramatic vision must be placed side by side with his praise for the composer's genuine achievements.[39] If Mallarmé admires the power and brilliance of Wagner's appropriation of the stage, he sees this act as an encroachment on the province of the poet, whose rights and duties Wagner has usurped (541). Quite apart from incidental qualifications, Mallarmé's "*Rêverie*" is directed, as Henri de Régnier has well said, "*contre cette captation par la musique dramatique, du vers et du geste, et contre sa substitution sur la scène à la poésie.*"[40] We are constantly reminded in Mallarmé's essay of the opposition of the musical composer and the poet, and it is through a poet's eyes that Wagner is presented. If Wagner professed to unite all of the arts into a single, total art work, Mallarmé nonetheless viewed his theory and technique as a means whereby "*la Musique pénètre et enveloppe le Drame*" (543). All of the arts would in fact come to be subordinated to music, and poetry would have only peripheral importance. Hence the presence in Mallarmé of "*un malaise que tout soit fait, autrement qu'en irradiant, par un jeu direct, du principe littéraire même*" (542).

As we shall see in our consideration of Mallarmé's views

of the music of poetry, the radical opposition between the poet and the musician rises from the very nature of their separate arts. It is possible that Mallarmé simply did not care for Wagner's music,[41] but his objections are those of a poet, and not merely those of a listener. His reservations apply not so much to Wagner as an artist, as to his formulation of the relationship of music to poetry.[42] It is noteworthy that Mallarmé was far more aware than any of his predecessors of the essentially anti-literary tendency of Wagner's theories;[43] the recognition of this bias, which would have been apparent at once from a reading of the major, untranslated treatises, testifies to the rigorous scrutiny with which Mallarmé examined Wagner's reformulation of dramatic art.

It is not easy to determine from the " *Rêverie* " alone precisely how well Mallarmé knew Wagner's work. In his letter to Dujardin in which he promises his manuscript for the August 8, 1885 number of the *Revue Wagnérienne* he declares, " Je n'ai jamais rien vu de Wagner ";[44] nevertheless, he had heard or read innumerable descriptions of Wagner's operas, and he displays some familiarity with them in his essay. His knowledge of Wagner's theories was certainly not first hand to any significant extent, but was probably derived mainly from Wyzewa, Dujardin, and others of the circle of the *Revue Wagnérienne*.[45] It is, of course, possible that Mallarmé might have acquired a more thorough and earlier knowledge of Wagner, principally through Baudelaire's essay, and even in early numbers of the *Revue Wagnérienne* there are a number of important citations from Wagner's " *Lettre sur la Musique*." Thus, the subordination in *Tristan und Isolde* of external action to " *mouvements intérieurs de l'âme* " was clearly described in a passage quoted by Dujardin.[46] Wagner's disparagement of poetry and his sharp separation of poetry and drama were set forth in an excerpt from his essay on Beethoven.[47] If Mallarmé did in fact come to his knowledge of Wagner's theories in the pages of the *Revue Wagnérienne*, it would seem that he read them with much more care than did Wagner's younger enthusiasts, and it is not difficult to understand why he did not altogether share their religious worship of the master of Bayreuth.

This reluctance to participate in the deification of Wagner dominates the conclusion of the "*Rêverie*." For while Mallarmé addresses Wagner as a true genius, he finds himself unable to join "*ceux qui . . . vont droit à l'édifice de ton Art, pour eux le terme du chemin*" (546). Nevertheless, this art will be a constant source of delight to the poet, even if he is not among the elect who kneel before the composer's shrine. The tone of reservation rising from the criticism of Wagner in the body of the essay is accompanied by a real sense of appreciation for the efforts of a fellow artist and a genuine admiration for Wagner's greatness. The two attitudes are in no way contradictory, and if Mallarmé's sense of separation from Wagner is at the center of the poet's reflections, the essay nevertheless gives evidence of a deep sense of spiritual kinship.

If, on the one hand, it is incorrect to exaggerate the "Wagnerianism" of Mallarmé's "*Rêverie*" and to describe it as "*peut-être le plus complet exposé de sa doctrine*," [48] it is also wrong to see in it a complete and total rejection of Wagner's vision of a synthesis of the arts.[49] Without overstating the importance of the "*Rêverie*" in the development of Mallarmé's aesthetic, it is clear that he emerged from his confrontation of Wagner with a new awareness of the interrelatedness of the arts in the theater. Even without attending a performance of Wagnerian opera, Mallarmé was able to distinguish between the alleged harmony of the arts in Wagner's theory, and the predominant role of music in his expression. Nonetheless, as his subsequent formulations of "*le rêve du Livre*" were to show, the values of Mallarmé's ideal art work came to reflect precisely those qualities he praised most highly in Wagner. His meditations on Wagner's art led him to a more personal formulation of a ritualistic theory of the drama,[50] a theory which relied on the values of mystery, suggestiveness, and atmospheric evocation, as well as on the interaction of the several arts, and which was to play a role of paramount importance in the symbolist drama. Even while pointing out Wagner's real inadequacies,

63

Mallarmé learned much from him. Wagner's cosmic vision, its limits but also its achievement, was a constant preoccupation of Mallarmé's during his own reformulation of the drama in the years following 1885.

There is no more convincing proof of the powerful imaginative impact of Wagner on Mallarmé than the famous " *Hommage*," a sonnet begun around September 1885 in response to the insistent request of Dujardin,[51] and published in the *Revue Wagnérienne* for January 8, 1886. The poem goes well beyond the " *Rêverie* " in its praise of Wagner's genius. His new art stands forth in magnificent relief against the decay of the old theater and the traditional modes of poetic expression.[52] It is reasonable in this context to see the " *principal pilier* " as Victor Hugo rather than the composer himself.[53] The climax of the poem is dominated by the imposing presence of the genius who has created a new art form:

> Le dieu Richard Wagner irradiant un sacre
> Mal tu par l'encre même en sanglots sibyllins.

The final line is perhaps an expression of the inadequacy of traditional literary expression in the face of Wagner's art, or it may simply evoke the contrast in the effects of music and written language. Mallarmé here retracts none of the reservations concerning Wagner's theories that he set forth in the " *Rêverie*," but neither does he mention them again. The object of the poem—homage to Wagner—itself precludes any overt criticism; while Mallarmé's ambivalent attitude was to persist, his view of the composer as an artist is, in this poem, one of unqualified admiration.

The dialog with Wagner on dramatic theory begun in the " *Rêverie* " was to be continued by the poet as a result of his own effort to revolutionize the theater in his essays in dramatic criticism of 1886-87. We have already seen that Mallarmé's principal objection to Wagner's aesthetic arose from the subordination of poetry to music in the classification of the arts. Among other objections was the charge that Wagner's survey of the arts of the theater had omitted the dance (541). Mallarmé's disagreement with Wagner on this point was of crucial importance to the poet, for it provided further evidence of the composer's glorification of music at the expense of all the other arts of the theater.

We find Mallarmé subsequently taking an even sharper attitude toward Wagner's view of the dance. In a letter of December 1886 to the Italian critic and popularizer of the symbolists, Vittorio Pica, the poet objects to the conception of the dance which Pica attributed to him in an article in the *Gazzetta Letteraria* of December 4:

> Je parle bien du Ballet qui mêle au Drame personnel pour y apporter un élément plus strictement allégorique, le ramène ainsi de l'histoire ou même de la légende à la poésie ou au mythe pur. Wagner a proscrit cette écriture merveilleuse et immédiatement significative de la danse, s'en tenant plus ou moins à quelque juxtaposition de Beethoven à Shakespeare (ainsi qu'il donne quelque part à entendre).[54]

It is one thing to claim that Wagner ignored the dance, and quite another to claim that he banned it. Mallarmé's concluding remarks suggest that he is not completely sure of precisely where in Wagner's writings this proscription is to be found, and this vagueness points again to the strong likelihood that Mallarmé derived his knowledge of Wagner largely, if not exclusively, from the pages of the *Revue Wagnérienne*.

The large gaps in the understanding of Wagner on the part of Mallarmé's young disciples should make one somewhat suspicious of the accuracy of the poet's charge. It is true that very little is said about the dance in the passages of Wagner that are cited in early issues of the *Revue Wagnérienne*; yet the subject is by no means ignored. Mallarmé seems to have formed his judgment hastily. Even without the aid of translations, Wagner's " *Lettre sur la Musique* " would have provided ample evidence of Wagner's keen interest in the dance as an art form. In his essay of 1861, Wagner emphasizes the role of the dance in the development of Greek music, and in no way disparages its contribution to melody or to dramatic performance. Indeed,

65

Wagner protests strongly against the proscription of the dance by the early Christians.[55] Primitive dance was for Wagner an essential part of dramatic action, strikingly different in this respect from the merely decorative role of the modern ballet.

In his major theoretical writings, Wagner clearly did not proscribe the dance, but he insisted that it be fused with the other primary elements of dramatic performance.[56] Like *Dichtkunst* and *Tonkunst*, *Tanzkunst* is not an independent art, separable from the total art work, but within this context it is necessary and indeed indispensable. Yet, if it is incorrect to claim that Wagner banned the dance in his vision of the ideal drama, it is clear that he had only stern condemnation for the modern ballet.[57] His conception of the dance is altogether different. From *Rienzi* to *Parsifal*, his works testify to a preoccupation with the dance, not as classical ballet, but in a looser, freer, more stridently emotional form of expression. The most celebrated instance is the " Venusberg Bacchanal " in the first act of *Tannhäuser*, of which the composer declared in a letter of April 10, 1860: "*nur der Tanz hier wirken und ausführen kann: aber welcher Tanz!*"[58] The Bacchanal is a reversion to what Wagner conceived of as a primitive and ritualistic celebration of passion, completely free of the artificiality of the ballet.

Mallarmé could have learned of Wagner's disparagement of the ballet from some of the early essays in the *Revue Wagnérienne*. Dujardin, in paraphrasing Wagner's disdain for the isolated and decorative character of modern opera and ballet, remarks: "La symphonie et le drame sont deux formes successives de la mélodie véritable, comme le ballet et l'opéra en sont les deux parodies."[59] Here as elsewhere, Wagner is making a sharp distinction between dance and ballet. It would have been accurate for Mallarmé to claim that Wagner had proscribed the ballet—and perhaps this is what the poet meant; but Mallarmé himself at times expressed reservations about the ballet that were very close indeed to those of Wagner. Like the composer, he protested against the literary appropriation of the dance by the classical ballet (312), and while on occasion Mallarmé seems to have genuine praise for ballet, there is no doubt that he preferred freer dance forms.[60] In this respect there is a large degree of similarity between the poet and the composer. Mallarmé's assertion, so often repeated, that "*Wagner a proscrit cette écriture merveilleuse et immédiatement significative de la danse*" must be viewed as an error based on partial and inadequate understanding. On the other hand, the charge itself is a strong expression of imagined if not of real differences and provides yet further evidence of the distance between Wagner's notion of total art and Mallarmé's awareness of the intrinsic values of the individual arts. It was inevitable that one objection of Mallarmé to Wagner's theories should lead to another. Quite apart from the merits of Mallarmé's charge, the very fact that he made it suggests once more that the poet's admiration for the composer's genius was seriously qualified when applied to his dramatic ideal.

From the moment that Mallarmé became aware of Wagner's sweeping and colossal vision of the possibilities of the music drama, the composer was vividly present in the reflections and aspirations of the poet. Mallarmé was torn between the imposing power of Wagner's genius and his own deeply felt reservations. His doubts and hesitations were never dispelled, and in the years following the "*Rêverie*" and the "*Hommage*," his mixed feelings toward Wagner were to assert themselves again and again. Thus, in an essay in dramatic criticism of 1887, he calls Wagner's art "*le plus compréhensif de ce temps*,"[61] but this praise must be seen in the perspective of the poet's view of the utter decay of the theater of his day. In his conversation with disciples and friends, Mallarmé sometimes spoke of Wagner with sincere admiration;[62] yet more often than not, particularly at the "*mardis*," his attitude constituted nothing less than a "*protestation contre l'ensemble de l'esthétique wagnérienne*."[63] Typical of the poet's disagreement is the report of the "*mardi*" of January 18, 1895, when he criticized Wagner severely for placing poetry, music, and the dance on the same plane in his theories and for giving music a preponderant and even exclusive importance.[64] Wagner, according to Mallarmé, had reduced the art of the poet to a position of distinct inferiority to music. In this context, we can readily appreciate Paul Valéry's description of the common effort of the symbolist poets: *"de reprendre à la musique leur bien."* [65]

Despite Mallarmé's defense of poetry against the claims of music, it is altogether possible that his persistent concern in the 1890's with the music of poetry and with the interrelations of the arts in the theater owed much to Wagner's example. The ambivalence in the poet's attitude continued to the very end of his life. At his deathbed was a copy of Wagner's *Beethoven* translated by Wyzewa,[66] evidently unread.[67] Here too we may see the same seemingly contradictory expression of imaginative sympathy and intellectual hesitation. Mallarmé's Wagnerian affiliations are real and important; yet they were exaggerated in his time as they are in ours.[68] Camille Mauclair could declare, *"il était un fervent wagnérien,"* [69] and Georges Rodenbach exclaimed, *"il adore Wagner"*;[70] yet these and countless other unqualified and uncritical remarks fail to take account of the complexities of Mallarmé's thought,[71] particularly in regard to those elements in his vision of a symbolist drama which follow from premises that are at sharp variance with the assumptions and aims of Wagner's art.

Before examining those elements in Mallarmé's dramatic theory that go beyond his concern with Wagner's values and limitations, we should consider the scope as well as the limits of Wagner's impact. The problems which the composer forced on the attention of the poet cannot be restricted to any single part of Mallarmé's mature reflections on the theater. Particularly in his ceaseless reformulations of "L'Œuvre" and "Le Livre," we shall see overtones, and more than overtones, of Wagnerian attitudes. Nevertheless, Wagner's impact is expressed not so much in the poet's unrealized personal ambitions, as in his probing examination of the theater in his time. His rejection of a drama of literal representation and his insistence on the internalization of action through suggestion and symbolization coincide markedly with Wagner's theory and practice. The ritualistic view of the drama, fusing art and religion, is another point of convergence of crucial importance. Even if these ideas did not originate in Mallarmé's thought as a result of the impact of Wagner, it can be said that the composer sustained and reinforced many of the poet's most cherished dreams and convictions.

On the other hand, it is wrong to ascribe exclusively or even primarily to Wagnerian influence similar attitudes which Mallarmé derived from a wide variety of sources. It has often been claimed that Mallarmé espoused the ideal of the synthesis of the arts in Wagnerian terms.[72] This may have been true for some of his disciples, but the union of the arts in the Wagnerian sense of total art was never a serious objective for Mallarmé himself.[73] To this ideal, Mallarmé opposed a rigorous purity of genre, fully in keeping with "*l'esprit français, strictement imaginatif et abstrait, donc poétique*" (544). Thus, the drama is essentially "*historique*"; the ballet, "*emblématique*." The two arts may reinforce one another; yet each must retain its individuality: "*Allier, mais ne confondre.*"[74] In place of the principle of the fusion of the separate arts into a new, total art work, Mallarmé asserts the supremacy of the poet, whose function it is to control the interplay of the arts in the theater.[75] In his evocation of the theater as it might become, he writes of the drama as a sacred rite drawing upon all of the arts, but under the aegis of poetry: "Notre seule magnificence, la scène, à qui le concours d'arts divers scellé par la Poésie attribue selon moi quelque caractère religieux ou officiel . . . ."[76] If there are elements of Wagner present here, there is also an essential opposition to his view of the interrelations of the arts.[77] Mallarmé's "synthetic" drama is not a new collective art work at all, but an interaction and mutual reinforcement of the separate arts, dominated by poetry.

From this standpoint, it is altogether fitting to describe Mallarmé's dramatic theory as poetic, as opposed to Wagner's, which we may call operatic. Within the development of the symbolist drama in Europe in the late nineteenth and early twentieth centuries, both attitudes are present, sometimes even in the work of the same playwright. In Mallarmé, however,

the operatic values in his dramatic theory are of little importance as part of his insistence on the supremacy of poetry. His
position is not unlike that of his master, Théodore de Banville.
Thus, in a letter of March 1896 to Émile Zola, thanking him
for a copy of his libretto, *Messidor*, Mallarmé points out that
he views "*le théâtre chanté et dansé sous un aspect très diffé-
rent.*" [78] He does not elaborate, but his other writings strongly
suggest that his view of the place of music in the theater was
in close accord with that of Banville.

It has been well said: "*le silence de Mallarmé jeune sur
Wagner . . . contraste éloquemment avec ses effusions pour
Banville.*" [79] This contrast is present in Mallarmé's later years
just as clearly as in his youth. His deification of poetry took
on meaning not only as a personal ideal, but as a glorification
of the image of the poet which Banville represented: "Nul
mieux ne représente maintenant le Poëte, l'invincible, classique
Poëte" (520). We have seen how strongly Banville inspired
Mallarmé's youthful dramatic efforts. In later life as well, Mallarmé's vision of what the drama could become was inspired
by his admiration for his master. The fact that the modern
theater, "*ce banal sacrilège,*" [80] in its absorption with realistic
representation, had rejected not only Banville's plays but also
the theater of fantasy and poetry which these plays exemplified,
did not alter Mallarmé's view. Banville's theory and expression
pointed to the theater as it might become, and in this respect it
is akin to Wagner's visionary aspirations.

It is the example of Banville and the force of the poetic
tradition which he represents that enable us to see more clearly
the difference between Wagner's total art and Mallarmé's
synthesis of the arts. For both Banville and Mallarmé, the
new theater was to embody a synthesis of the resources of
poetry and music, mime and dance, in "*l'Ode, dramatisée par
des effets de coupe savants.*" [81] The "*ode à plusieurs voix,*" as
Mallarmé characterized Banville's *Le Forgeron: Scènes Héroïques*, is to be recited, rather than performed in the manner of
anecdotal drama. Its spaciousness and flexibility, not simply in
the exploration of the hidden mysteries of existence, but in the

interplay of the artistic resources at its disposal, free the drama from the confines of realistic representation.[82] In this respect, Mallarmé's ideal is similar to Wagner's: both are festive and ceremonial, both constitute an effort to go beyond "*le théâtre, borné ou incapable tout seul de répondre à de très subtils instincts*" (335). Yet, the poet is careful to emphasize the differences: the dramatized ode is opposed not only to the traditional theater, but to Wagnerian opera as well.

The distance between the ideal of Mallarmé and the Wagnerian total art stems from the opposition of poetry to music as the central, controlling element in the drama. We have seen an adumbration of this contrast in the "*Rêverie*" on Wagner, for the elimination of anecdote is at sharp variance with the composer's insistence on the primacy of legend within a musical setting. The theater Mallarmé envisages is not the music-drama, but "*la Fable, vierge de tout, lieu, temps et personne sus, . . . c'est à dire, un Poëme, l'Ode*" (544-45). The contrast is developed even more sharply in the reflections on Banville's *Le Forgeron*: "Chez Wagner . . . ce n'est plus dans l'acceptation correcte le théâtre . . . mais la vision légendaire qui suffit sous le voile des sonorités et s'y mêle." The triumph of Banville, on the other hand, consists precisely in the fact that his art is "*littéraire dans l'essence.*"[83] The same opposition of poetic and operatic values that is evident in Banville's attitude toward Wagner is present in Mallarmé's position.

Indeed, nowhere is Mallarmé's vision of the theater more programmatic than in his discussion of Banville. Almost the whole of the chronicle in the *Revue Indépendante* for June 1887 is devoted to a glowing account of *Le Forgeron*, which provided personal compensation for Mallarmé for the absence of poetry in the theater.[84] Banville's title page carries the heading, "*Poème Inédit,*" and we may assume that Mallarmé liked the poem precisely because it was not intended for stage presentation: "*Spectacle intellectuel qui me passionne*" (334). *Le Forgeron* appealed to Mallarmé not simply because it was the work of a poet whom he admired, but because it evoked an antique and pastoral setting very close to that of Banville's *Diane au Bois* and *La Pomme*, or Mallarmé's *Faune*. The slight and simple narrative is the account of Venus' choice of a husband. In turn, she rejects Bacchus, Apollo, Jupiter, and Mercury, for Vulcan, and their union is the climax of the work. Banville's dramatic poem can be read as an allegory, with the marriage of Venus and Vulcan symbolizing the wedding of beauty and creative force. The realm of Olympus is an analog of the world of human events, and the sustained praise of Venus is in fact a hymn to poetry. Mallarmé must have taken particular delight in the sensuous depiction of the ancient Greek pastoral atmosphere, wherein Jupiter evokes "*le faune lascif et le chevreau qui grimpe/ . . . sur le neigeux Olympe.*"[85] Yet, literary associations alone would not account for Mallarmé's rapt admiration. *Le Forgeron* is not only a testimony of a poet's genius, "*un être à part, primitif et buvant tout seule à une source occulte et éternelle*";[86] it is an expression of the play as a book, "performed" in the theater of the imagination:

> Quelle représentation! le monde y tient; un livre, dans notre main, s'il énonce quelque idée auguste, supplée à tous les théâtres, non par l'oubli qu'il en cause mais les rappelant impérieusement, au contraire (334).

The theater of the mind does not displace or substitute for the physical theater, but enlarges and spiritualizes its resources. Banville's art is completely assimilated into the ideal of a symbolist drama: suggestive, imaginative, musical, and above all poetic. The evocative magic and varied rhythm of Banville's poetry, like all poetry, carries its own musicality, "*littéraire dans l'essence.*" In place of literal anecdote drawn from everyday life, the drama consists of broad and abstract symbolic generalization: the spectacle of "*la femme ou beauté humaine*" wedded to the creator of masterpieces (334). Here, for Mallarmé, is a concrete exemplification of the dramatic ode, a poem for an ideal theater, incorporating the interrelation of all the arts, but with poetry at the center of the drama.

The vision of the drama which Mallarmé found implicit in *Le Forgeron* has very little to do with the Wagnerian ideal.

From a literary standpoint, the tone and spirit of Banville's dramatic poem are remarkably close to the comedies of Musset. The sense of fantasy and caprice, the subtle and playful awareness of nuances of feeling, and the lively wit and repartee are all part of a literary conception of drama such as is suggested by the very title, "*Un Spectacle dans un fauteuil.*" Perforce, this is not a drama for the mass theater-going public, and yet Mallarmé saw in *Le Forgeron*, "*malgré l'origine classique*," a drama which "*par-dessus tout émerveillera le Peuple*" (336). Mallarmé's view of the collective and religious values of Banville's art is based upon an analogy with the ancient Greek drama: as a result of the recitation of the dramatic ode to the masses, Mallarmé hoped for profound social and philosophical consequences.[87] These hopes have little to do with Banville's modest poem, for they express a lifelong dream of cosmic and universal drama whose nearest analogs may be found in Shakespeare or Goethe and which may have been reinforced by Wagner's art as well. Thus, even though *Le Forgeron* is much closer to Musset and the French classical drama than to Wagner, it would be wrong to insist on too rigorous an antithesis. In Mallarmé's subsequent elaboration of the ideal drama, in his plans and projects as well as in his dramatic criticism, we can see elements of the theaters of Banville and Wagner side by side, assimilated and fused into a new and highly personal synthesis. If Mallarmé had written a drama late in life, it may well have taken a form resembling Banville's "*Scènes Héroïques*," but the theatrical composition on which he meditated cannot be viewed apart from his ceaseless preoccupation with Wagner and with the reformation of the drama.

The lofty and impassioned idealism which animated Mallarmé's reëxamination of the theater clearly did not impose a complete abandonment of the physical stage. Mallarmé enjoyed all kinds of theatrical performances and was able to accept them on their own terms. He took a lively interest in the Théâtre de Valvins, founded by Paul and Victor Margueritte in 1881. Their cousin, the poet's daughter Geneviève, played light comic roles, such as Banville's Nérine, and Mallarmé participated as "*souffleur et metteur en scène.*" [88] The repertoire was made up of light, short plays taken from *commedia dell' arte*, from Musset, or from Banville, with interspersed performances of mime or recitation. The Théâtre de Valvins seems to have captivated the poet completely; it may well lie at the source of his subsequent "*obsession d'un théâtre encore réduit et miniscule ou lointain,* . . . *intime gala pour soi.*" [89] The ideal of a small and intimate coterie theater accorded well with Mallarmé's symbolist aesthetic, but his direct participation in the modest productions at Valvins may have also inspired his larger social ambitions. Paul Margueritte reports that after rehearsals, Mallarmé would engage in discussions of the destiny of the theater, in which he set forth the vision of the poet taking the stage before the attentive masses, revealing beauty to the unlettered public.[90] Mallarmé displayed genuine ability to write for such an audience in a lively and spirited popular idiom, as in the "*Monologue de Pathelin*" composed for a performance of the farce at Valvins (182-84). The style is in sharp contrast to the poetry Mallarmé was writing at the same time; it suggests that his early plans for a drama of popular entertainment were by no means unsuited to his talents. Nevertheless, the vision of a completely different mode of dramatic expression soon came to dominate his involvement in the theater. Although at first glance, Mallarmé's ideal drama is removed from the slight and uncomplicated performances at Valvins, the poet's close participation in dramatic productions undoubtedly contributed to enlarge his awareness of the possibilities of the stage.

The dramatic projects of Mallarmé's early years may have been altered or interrupted from time to time, but it is not likely that they were ever abandoned. In a letter of September 10, 1885 to Dujardin, Mallarmé insists that he has no time for contributions to periodicals because of his work on the draft of a play: "Des études de Drame, comme je le rêve. . . ." [91] A return to drama at this time may have been an immediate result of the meditations on Wagner, but Mallarmé's dramatic aspirations go back, as we have seen, to the very beginning of his literary activity. It is not so much the ambition to create drama that follows from the poet's interest in Wagner, as it is his redefinition of the concept of L'Œuvre, which he initially set forth almost twenty years earlier. It is in intimate relation to this concept that Mallarmé's mature dramatic theories and aspirations must be viewed.

The description of the poet's "Grand Œuvre" in his famous autobiographical letter to Verlaine of November 1885 is in the same terms which we have found in the annunciatory letters of 1867. In his "*Autobiographie*," Mallarmé laments the immense gulf between his ambition and his accomplishment: while he has dreamed, "*avec une patience d'alchimiste*," of the great work that will crown his life of dedication, he has given himself over, in his writing, to "*des inspirations de hasard*." He tells Verlaine of his true ambition, a book "*en maints tomes, un livre qui soit un livre, architectural et prémédité. . . . J'irai plus loin, je dirai le Livre, persuadé qu'au fond il n'y en a qu'un* . . ." (662-63). Mallarmé has not altogether abandoned his initial conception of L'Œuvre as the ensemble of a poet's compositions, but the mystical and philosophical implications have been carried even further than they were during the first year of elaboration. Mallarmé's incorporation of all of literature and, indeed, of the universe itself is an expression of a deeply-rooted traditional mysticism.[92] Yet, while many earlier mystics portrayed the universe as a book, Mallarmé reversed the relationship and described the book as an embodiment of the universe.[93] It is as an expression of this symbolic relationship that he defines the "*seul devoir du poète*" as "*L'explication orphique de la Terre*." The poetic act is itself a part of the "*rêve du Livre*," whose rhythm and material form "*se juxtapose aux équations de ce rêve, ou Ode*" (663). Does Mallarmé's view of the ode in this context correspond to that of Banville, and does it reflect the subsequent opposition of the "*Ode, dramatisée*" to the Wagnerian synthesis? The letter to Verlaine provides no explicit answer, but Mallarmé's subsequent reflections clearly indicate that the mystical notion of "*Le Livre*" which sustains and directs all literature includes the drama as well as all other literary forms. Mallarmé was completely serious when he

75

declared to Huret in 1891: "*le monde est fait pour aboutir à un beau livre*" (872).[94]

There can be no doubt that Mallarmé's "Grand Œuvre" or "*Livre*" came to be closely associated with his dramatic aspirations. In a letter to Vittorio Pica, probably written in November 1886,[95] Mallarmé declares his faith in the power of literature to bring forth "*un Théâtre, dont les représentations seront le vrai culte moderne; un Livre, explication de l'homme, suffisant à nos plus beaux rêves.*" The ritualistic function of this theater will be fulfilled presumably through its literary as well as its presentational qualities, but Mallarmé's concluding remarks point to the futility of attempting any precise description. The "*explication de l'homme*" is also "*L'explication orphique de la Terre*" with which the "Grand Œuvre" is coexistent: "*Cette œuvre existe, tout le monde l'a tentée sans la savoir; ... Montrer cela et soulever un coin du voile de ce que peut être pareil poëme, est dans un isolement mon plaisir et ma torture*" (876). Just as Mallarmé suggested in his letter to Verlaine that, at best, he could not hope to produce the totality of the "Grand Œuvre," "*mais à en montrer un fragment d'exécuté,*" so in his letter to Pica, there is no prospect of complete realization of the poet's ideal. The letter of 1886 proves, however, that in the year following the composition of the "*Autobiographie,*" if not earlier, the dream of the great work came to include the art of drama along with poetry. The theater of the poet's vision requires no visible stage: it is a simultaneous expression of book, poem, and play, such as Mallarmé may have conceived underlying his *Un Coup de Dés.*[96] The doubts and hesitations of the poet before the magnitude of his task should not suggest that he viewed his dream as mere fantasy. From the very outset, he projected his hopes into the future, and perhaps even in 1886, he felt that "*le vrai culte moderne*" could emerge in the theater only through the efforts of a more powerful dramatic genius than he could ever hope to become. Yet, the ambition was not merely utopian: it was the abiding preoccupation of the poet in the last years of his life, and it shaped virtually everything that he came to write about the theater.

The publication in 1957 of *Le " Livre " de Mallarmé*, edited by Jacques Scherer, makes it absolutely clear that the poet envisioned his "Grand Œuvre" as a composition for dramatic performance. Even though Mallarmé did not publish his notes and drafts, he talked about his plans to his young friends. Francis Vielé-Griffin reports that at a *"mardi"* in January 1887, Mallarmé spoke of *"l'Œuvre à venir"* as a dramatic work.[97] Henri de Régnier described Mallarmé's "Œuvre" not simply as an ideal but as a definite composition,[98] while Vittorio Pica in an essay of 1891 was even more explicit: "Mallarmé travaille continuellement à un drame poétique, destiné à être l'incarnation suprême de son effort artistique." [99] Pica subsequently qualifies his remarks, recognizing that for Mallarmé any literary work can partake of the qualities of drama; [100] yet it is altogether possible that here, as elsewhere, the Italian critic simply paraphrased a statement made by Mallarmé in a letter to him. In any case, we cannot accept at face value everything which Mallarmé is reported to have said, and perhaps did say, concerning his "Grand Œuvre." René Ghil's elaborate account of twenty volumes points, as Edouard Dujardin suggests, to Mallarmé's love of playful exaggeration rather than to any seriously conceived plan.[101] The poet himself in 1895 alluded to *"le magique concept de l'Œuvre,"* not as his own unique property or aspiration, but as an embodiment of the ideal of absolute poetry imposing itself on all young poets of the day (367). In this broadly symbolic sense, Mallarmé's poetic vision embraces not only all of literature, but also the universe, itself a vast poem, an expression of the ideal work of art; however, in a narrower sense, on the plane of artistic creation, we may safely assert that the poet's concept of L'Œuvre was dramatic and theatrical as well as literary.[102]

Just as the notion of an ideal work of art was to shape Mallarmé's view of the future of the drama, so, conversely, the vision of L'Œuvre must be seen in the multiple perspective of the poet's late dramatic theory. As his manuscript notes make clear, all of literature for Mallarmé came to be described in theatrical terms.[103] At one point in the notes, he asserts:

"*identité du Livre et de la Pièce.*" [104] Since reading is a means of evoking an imaginary theater, the qualities of dramatic expression are residual properties of the ideal work of art: "Le Livre implique le théâtre." [105] Maeterlinck, with his evocation of dream, mystery, and wonder, "*inséra le théâtre au livre!*" (329). The same claim could be made for a dramatic poem like Banville's *Le Forgeron.* Banville himself, in his despair over the dominance of Scribe, "*pitoyable écrivain,*" and the exclusion of poetry from the theater, anticipated Mallarmé's formulation when he wrote: "Les grandes œuvres dramatiques ne demeurent au théâtre et n'y persistent que par le Livre." [106] For Mallarmé "*le Drame*" and "*le Livre*" are identical; we can make no sharp separation between the two, for clearly Mallarmé made none.

This interpenetration of the play and the book is reflected in the poet's plans for the representation or performance of his composition. These were elaborated in great detail. The "*theater*" was to include only a single actor, the poet, "*unique récitant,*" fully in keeping with Mallarmé's notion of "performance":

Séances
de Lectures du Drame
et de l'Hymne.[107]

The performer was to be Mallarmé himself,[108] who would recite for a select audience of eight or, at most, twenty-four persons.[109] Along with this intimate representation, Mallarmé envisaged that publication of his work would provide a more suitable means of diffusion than could professional performance all over France. Although the poet despaired over the limitations inherent in the physical theater, he felt he would receive from an elite an imaginative sympathy that the mass public could hardly be expected to provide. Though intimate, Mallarmé's poetic recitation was envisaged as a public ceremony and a means of revealing spiritual truths to the masses. This aspiration seems to go back at least as far as Mallarmé's participation in the Théâtre de Valvins: "Un de ses vœux," reports Paul Margueritte, "était que le poète, en des salles immenses, devant des foules attentives, prononçât les phrases lapidaires de l'enseignement esthétique, d'où tout découlait. Seul, le poète sachant, affirmait-il, révéler la beauté, source de vertu parfaite, aux masses."[110] This view, which is reinforced in many of the later critical essays, is far removed indeed from the notion of *l'art pour l'art* sometimes attributed to Mallarmé. It provides an interesting anticipation of the desire of W. B. Yeats to bring together the poetry of the coterie and the poetry of the folk. Mallarmé's view of his relationship to his audience suggests that the plans for the performance of "Hamlet and the wind," described to George Moore in 1876, were not altogether in jest. However, in spite of Mallarmé's concern with the details of physical production of his ideal drama, we cannot consider his *"Livre"* as more than fragmentary jottings, far more interesting to the student of Mallarmé's aesthetics than to the critic or historian of the drama. All the same, these notes point to a profound endeavor on the part of the poet to clarify his objectives through illustration. His manuscript notes do not describe the only theater possible, but constitute rather a partial and indeed modest indication of the potentialities of the poet's dramatic vision.

The notion of *"Le Livre"* in Mallarmé's thought has been well described as a *"système des Beaux-Arts,"* embodying qualities of poetry, theater, ballet, symphony, and the other arts as well.[111] In the light of Mallarmé's unusual interest in the interrelations of the arts, it is not difficult to understand the readiness with which many critics and scholars identify Mallarmé's *"Œuvre"* and Wagner's *Gesamtkunstwerk*.[112] Our previous examination of Mallarmé's critique of Wagner should rule out any description of the poet's dramatic vision in precise Wagnerian terms; yet, on the other hand, we cannot agree with the opposite view that the poet owes little or nothing to Wagner in his conception of dramatic art.[113] The problem is complicated by the many partial or inaccurate interpretations of Wagner which Mallarmé read in the pages of the *Revue Wagnérienne*, for here too we find attitudes and values that are close indeed to the poet's dramatic ideal.

In the same issue of the *Revue Wagnérienne* which contained Mallarmé's "*Richard Wagner: Rêverie d'un Poëte français*," we may see in Dujardin's account of "Bayreuth" an evocation of cosmic drama in language strikingly suggestive of that subsequently employed by Mallarmé:

> . . . le Livre, ce tout puissant suggestif de l'Idée, ce Livre qui contenait son Œuvre de Poésie et de Théologie,—Wagner le lisait, l'impérieux créateur, et, seul, dans le calme silence de son rêve, parcourant des yeux les pages multiples, et des yeux suivant les Signes,—la lettre, la note et le trait,—il voyait et il entendait, manifestement suggérés par les Signes, vivre en lui, en le merveilleux et suprême théâtre de son Imagination, le drame réel et symbolique.[114]

It is very possible that in this passage, Mallarmé's friend and disciple has drawn together images and phrases dear to the poet and perhaps frequently employed by him. In any event, it is reasonable to suppose that Dujardin found at Bayreuth confirmation of the values and aspirations that Mallarmé's young disciple had brought there; it would not be the first occasion on which Wagner was transformed into a symbolist. Nevertheless, quite apart from the validity of Dujardin's interpretation of the composer, there can be no doubt that Mallarmé read these lines and saw in them a profound similarity to his own vision of the theater of the future. The metaphor of the Book of the Universe as the primal source of poetic revelation is, we have seen, altogether traditional in mystical and occult speculation, but the concern with dream, mystery, and suggestiveness in Wagner's art is described essentially from a symbolist standpoint. Dujardin's rhapsodic evocation is itself far from clear, more akin to a *poème en prose* than to a descriptive essay; yet if we were to substitute the name of Mallarmé for that of Wagner in the above passage, it would be difficult indeed to find any large measure of difference. Only, perhaps, in the final allusion to "*le drame réel et symbolique*," reminiscent of Baudelaire's account of the dissipation of reverie and wonder and the culmination of the drama in "*la pleine clairvoyance*,"[115] may we

find an intimation of a significant difference between Mallarmé
and Wagner. The poet's long and sustained meditation on the
possibilities of the drama brought him to an integration of genres
wherein " *Théâtre*," " *Drame*," " *Mystère*," and " *Hymne* " were
all aspects of a larger underlying reality, " *Le Livre*." [116] If the
poet's evocation of " *un opéra sans accompagnement ni chant,
mais parlé* " is an expression of a profound disagreement with
Wagner's view of the relationship of poetry to music,[117] it is
nonetheless clear that even while attacking Wagner, Mallarmé
came to borrow from him. The distinction between poetic
and operatic conceptions in the late nineteenth century is far
more a matter of emphasis than of absolute separation. Even
if we cannot consider Mallarmé's dream of a great art work as
a flat application of Wagnerian principles, there can be no
doubt that Wagner contributed directly and indirectly to the
reformulation of " L'Œuvre " in Mallarmé's later years. Despite
his very real and important reservations, Mallarmé appreciated
the aims and impulses underlying Wagner's gigantic enterprise
and recognized a large area of community with the composer,
even while rejecting some of his most crucial assumptions. Mallarmé's dramatic theory was largely a personal expression; yet
we cannot divorce it from the contemporary formulations on
which he drew. Shakespeare and Goethe, Banville and Wagner
weave in and out of his pages in an uneasy alliance. In the
last analysis, the vision of the theater which Mallarmé came to
formulate was of his own making. It is not the sources of the
poet's thought which are of first importance, but their incorporation into a personal synthesis which came to be of compelling
importance in shaping a significant area of the modern theater.

It would be well for us to keep in mind the distinction
between Mallarmé's view of his own capacities in the realization of his plans, and his notion of what the theater may in time
become.[118] More than one of his closest followers considered
his vision of " L'Œuvre " " *par définition irréalisable*." [119] Our
present knowledge of Mallarmé's notes and drafts lends strong
support to this conviction; yet we cannot condemn the poet
for his failures of realization. In the theater there were others

who sought to give Mallarmé's aspirations exemplification and substance. The resources of dramatic expression which the symbolist poets and playwrights came to explore were defined and illuminated most completely in Mallarmé's dramatic criticism, in essays which, like the critical writings of Baudelaire, are themselves a creative act.

IV

THE VISION OF A NEW THEATER

FROM 1885 TO THE END OF HIS LIFE, Mallarmé meditated and wrote on the theater. The essays and prose poems which the poet contributed to the literary reviews that clamored for his work, and which he subsequently collected in his *Divagations*, constitute a rich and complex statement of a highly original theory of drama. It is not Mallarmé's indebtedness to such vital forces in his development as Wagner or Banville which is of primary interest, but rather the ways in which he goes beyond them to break new ground. The "*Notes sur le théâtre*" which he contributed for several months to the *Revue Indépendante* demonstrate the poet's sensitivity and depth as a critic of the drama, and it is in his criticism far more than in his dramatic compositions, written or projected, that his most far-reaching contribution to the theater was to be made.

In retrospect, Mallarmé considered his essays in the *Revue Indépendante* as programmatic, part of "*une campagne dramatique*," an effort to change the theater, not merely to describe it.[1] Yet, in order to reshape the theater of his day, Mallarmé had to come to know it, and this meant attending all kinds of dramatic performances. The physical demands of the "*Notes sur le théâtre*" were exhausting, and doubly so because the Paris theatrical season of 1886-87 was not a particularly distinguished one. It provided ample illustration of the dominant obsession with "*l'universel reportage*" which the poet

83

saw in every area of contemporary writing (857). Scribe, Sardou, Dumas fils, Zola, and their confreres dominated the stage, relieved only by occasional revivals of classics such as Mounet-Sully's Hamlet, or by performances of pantomime or dance. Mallarmé's essays provide a valuable record of the theatrical year, but far more important, they constitute a demand for a total reorientation of the drama.

We must make a sharp distinction between the poet's view of the theater as he found it and his vision of the theater as it might become. Mallarmé's critique moves between two poles: the "*art si grossier* . . . *si abject*," as Gautier had described it,[2] and the ideal theater which Mallarmé strove to bring about. He had little sympathy for the drama of realistic prose, to which one responds "*comme par un* Ce n'est pas moi dont il est ici question."[3] Most of the plays he felt obliged to see are, he insists, not worth talking about. They are part of the "*banal sacrilège*" of the separation of drama from poetry. Mallarmé was well aware of the role played by public taste in the degradation of the stage. The theater of realistic prose he describes as "*temple d'un culte factice*";[4] but it is still a temple, even when desecrated: "*le grand art quand même!*" Mallarmé found the theater of literal representation tedious and dull, "*où chacun veut être dans le secret de quelque chose ne fût-ce que de la redite perpétuelle.*"[5] And yet, he could appreciate the interest which others might have in a realistic portrayal of individual or social experience. He had high praise for Zola's dramatic adaptation of *La Curée*[6] and was quite ready to accept the traditional "*théâtre de mœurs*,"[7] provided that it be taken on its own terms and not as a final expression of the possibilities of the drama. The poetic theater represented for Mallarmé the "other" theater, suggested here and there on the contemporary stage, but still awaiting the establishment of new attitudes and values for its realization. The easy and empty drama of mass entertainment, "*l'art officiel qu'on peut aussi appeler vulgaire*,"[8] was not to be supplanted overnight; but a beginning could be made by providing a sense of direction and by pointing to attitudes and techniques that would help to initiate the change.

It is as part of this effort that Mallarmé's dramatic theory must be understood.

Mallarmé's ideal theater is a symbolist drama, an expression of the same principles and values shaping and directing symbolist poetry. The separation of the drama from literal reality is absolute: "Le Théâtre est d'essence supérieure." [9] The present low estate of the stage has nothing to do with its inherent greatness. In its origin and destiny, drama is a sacred and mysterious rite, a suggestion or evocation of the hidden spiritual meaning of existence; it is an act of common participation and mutual involvement before " la majestueuse ouverture sur le mystère dont on est au monde pour envisager la grandeur." [10] This mystery is revealed indirectly, through dream and reverie, and in a language of rich musicality and allusiveness. " Remplacez Vaudeville par Mystère," [11] Mallarmé declares, in answer to Gautier's appeal for a return to spectacle. The mystery of drama resides not only in its language and gesture, but also in its embodiment of the ideal, its reflection of ultimate spiritual truth.

Thus, for Mallarmé the drama is not the expression of the experiences of any particular man, but rather " de la Passion de l'Homme ": [12] man in his spiritual and divine character, and not in his material and accidental state of being. [13] In this abstract and typical representation, the poet sees the union of the drama of personal heroism on the one hand and of impersonal mystery on the other: the fusion of theater and hymn. [14] In his highly personal reformulation of the drama, Mallarmé is not concerned with the details of the " explication de l'homme," but rather with the spiritual attitudes and values that the new theater will express: the primacy of mystery, dream, and imaginative vision, projected beyond any particular time or circumstance. [15] The magic and mystery of the theater reside within its very substance, as an evocation of the absolute, embracing the destiny of all humanity. In this sense, Mallarmé's ritual drama is the means of the propagation of a new religion, a secularization of the liturgy and rite of ancient dramatic performances.

This vision of a ceremonial theater is in fact a configuration of elements derived from a variety of sources: Greek drama, the medieval liturgical drama, Shakespeare, Wagner, Banville and the tradition of poetic drama, and the Catholic Mass. Mallarmé saw the theater of both the past and the future as a temple, wherein actor and spectator participate in a sacred rite.[16] Henri de Régnier fittingly described Mallarmé's theater as " *quelque chose d'analogue peut-être aux nobles fêtes théâtrales de la Grèce, une sorte de spectacle à la fois national, religieux et humain, auditif et visuel, en même temps que métaphysique, et où l'homme eût assisté à une célébration, non point réaliste mais fictive et emblématique de la vie et de lui-même.*"[17] We have seen that the Greek view of dramatic representation as an act of collective spiritual involvement dominated the Wagnerian *Bühnenfestspiel* and the theater at Bayreuth. For Mallarmé as well, the stage was invested with the solemnity and dedication of worship: " Mystère, autre que représentatif et que, je dirai, grec, Pièce, office " (393). The spectacle of the Catholic Mass was for Mallarmé the nearest analog of this liturgical conception. The audience participates in an act of mass communion, not for the sake of literal understanding, but rather as a celebration of a sacred mystery. Mallarmé's notion of " *Mystère* " is in many ways suggestive of medieval liturgical drama.[18] The presence of mystery transforms the audience into a community sharing a common awareness of the spirituality and wonder of the universe.

The mystical premises and overtones of Mallarmé's symbolist theory of drama should not obscure its profound social implications. For all of his hostility to the realistic or naturalistic drama of the day, Mallarmé shared with Zola and his contemporaries a deep concern for the moral and spiritual values of the masses.[19] The opposition of symbolist and naturalist drama is by no means as absolute as is sometimes assumed. Mallarmé saw the drama as fulfilling a state function, patriotic as well as liturgical.[20] He viewed the stage as a means of national education, " *la mise en scène de la religion d'état,*" the expression of a civic as well as a mystical cult (396). If the origins of the ideal drama are religious and ceremonial, the end is secular, in the triumphal evocation *"de Patrie, ou d'Honneur, de Paix"* (394). It is important to take full account of the repeated insistence of Mallarmé on the *rapports* of literature and society. As the poet declared to Jules Huret: *" dans une société sans stabilité, sans unité, il ne peut se créer d'art stable, d'art définitif "* (866). The full splendor and magnificence of the drama can be recovered only in a society *" où aurait sa place la gloire dont les gens semblent avoir perdu la notion "* (869). If the modern poet is *" en grève devant la société "* (870), this does not mean that his art is without social consequences. Both in its immediate and in its long-range effects, the drama for Mallarmé is an act of collective involvement, moving beyond mere entertainment or purely personal experiences, to embrace the deepest spiritual aspirations of both the individual and society.

Mallarmé's notion of *" Mystère "* is no mere abstraction. In *La Musique et les Lettres*, the poet places this concept at the very center of *" cette célébration de la poésie"*: *" appelez-là Mystère ou n'est-ce pas le contexte évolutif de l'Idée "* (653). Mystery is a reflection of *" l'Idée,"* the realm of pure spirituality, made particular and concrete in theatrical presentation. In the notes for his vast dramatic composition, Mallarmé clarifies this concept when he declares that Mystery and Drama, Drama and Mystery *" ne sont que même chose retournées présentant l'un en dehors ce que l'autre cache en dedans."* [21] In subsequent diagrams and notes, some of which became incorporated with the plans for *Igitur,* the poet set forth an elaborate schematization of this interrelationship: [22]

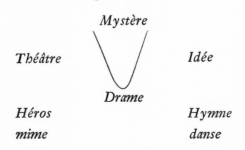

Clearly, "*Mystère*" for Mallarmé is not a mere reproduction of the medieval religious drama. It is coexistent with the art of drama and, indeed, with all literature. Just as Baudelaire insisted that we can apprehend the spirituality of the universe only through the mysteries of "*l'analogie*," so Mallarmé declares in "*Le Mystère dans les Lettres*," "Il doit y avoir quelque chose d'occulte au fond de tous" (383). The complex allusiveness of drama, its broad symbolic and cosmic implications as well as its necessary obscurity, is part of the conditions of all artistic experience. Yet, the incarnation of "*Mystère*" in "*Drame*" takes the form of a synthesis of the spiritual and the histrionic properties of ritualistic celebration: an idea, but also a performance, a fusion of action and incantation, mime and dance. Concretely as well as in its ideological premises, Mallarmé's vision of what the drama can become represents a total transformation of the theater, a return to the rudimentary elements of the drama in their pristine simplicity.

The reductive and elemental character of Mallarmé's dramatic theory is most apparent in his emphasis on the detheatricalization of the stage. As a consequence of the debasement of the theater in his time, the poet came to feel, at least at times, that the true value of a play could never be expressed in performance, but only through the medium of the printed page. We have seen that "*Le Livre*" for Mallarmé also constitutes a mode of dramatic expression, wherein the action is directed not so much to the senses of the spectator as to the mind or inner eye. Mallarmé's preference for closet drama is deeply rooted.[23] In his early attempts to compose drama, he viewed the theater in intimate association with poetry. It is useful to recall his intent in the composition of the *Faune* "Intermède": "*je veux conserver toute la poésie de mes œuvres lyriques, mon vers même, que j'adapte au drame.*"[24] The separation of poetry from the theater—the indifference of the stage to the role of language—issued in the poet's rejection of the purely theatrical elements of the drama.

In this respect, Mallarmé's attitude toward the theater is essentially the same as that of the English Romantics, most of whom considered a play read as superior to a play acted.[25] The resemblance is not fortuitous. Mallarmé was well aware of the plight of poetic drama across the channel, where Byron, Shelley, and their successors had been forced to create a theater "*fait des majestueux fantômes*" and constituting a "*fête idéale*" (702). It is in this context that the poet praises Swinburne's verse tragedy, *Erechtheus*, in a review of 1876. Swinburne's play, like those of his predecessors, is part of that theater "*dont on n'est le spectateur que chez soi, un tome ouvert ou les yeux fermés.*" It is the same notion of theater that was to reappear in Mallarmé's critical essays ten years later, and it may be a direct reflection of his reading of the critical essays of the English Romantics, whose work he knew well.

The gradual reduction of the "*Drame*" to "*Le Livre*" is itself part of Mallarmé's transference of visible action to the realm of the invisible.[26] The physical theater was not merely corrupt; it was, at least at times, utterly superfluous. With the passage of time, Mallarmé, like Banville before him, came to place increased emphasis on "*Le Livre*" rather than the "*Drame*" as the embodiment of the art of drama.[27] The reduction of the audience, to a single person at its extreme point,[28] went hand in hand with the virtual abandonment of the physical theater and the elimination of the acting group. The presence in "*Le Livre*" of only a single actor—the poet—precluded any dialog. There is perhaps a trace of plot action in Mallarmé's plans for the substance of his work, but the plans provide no more than the barest outline.[29] Anecdote went the same way as character in the poet's vision of performance in "*séances de lecture reglées comme un cérémonial.*"[30]

In his essay of 1895, "*Quant au Livre*," Mallarmé's image of the poet as actor was extended to embrace all of literature, not merely his own dramatic vision. The writer is in fact an actor, "*spirituel histrion,*" performing in an ideal theater: "*un Lieu se présente, scène, majoration devant tous du spectacle de Soi*" (370). The frequency and vividness of theatrical metaphor in Mallarmé's description of the writer's art suggest a lively histrionic imagination accompanying the projection of the poet as actor. If we assume a close relationship between "*Le Livre*" and Banville's dramatic ode, we may see the "*intime gala pour soi*" as the poet's act of performance, through recitation, as well as an account of the way in which the poet as spectator assimilates and inwardly transforms the plays which he sees performed. Banville's dramatic poem, *Le Forgeron*, "*Spectacle intellectuel qui me passionne*," [31] is in fact *performed* in Mallarmé's imagination. Its performance is a testimony of the grandeur of the theater of the mind.

This assertion of the sweep and magnificence of invisible representation as opposed to the poverty and the false intimacy of the contemporary stage is an insistent note in Mallarmé's observations on the drama. In a letter of April 1898 to Emile Verhaeren, he has no regret that *Les Aubes* is not to be produced. The play, like all great drama, will remain part of the theater of our deepest spiritual experience: [32]

> . . . reservée au seul théâtre de nous-mêmes, qui exige pour la donner, en son prodige, l'afflux de toutes nos somptuosités vitales et de la magnifique veille de la pensée: là seulement, où nous sommes tragiques devant les destins, au plus pur, au plus amer, au plus glorieux de chacun, peut s'installer, même pour une jouissance d'art, cet échange supérieur ou grandiose de cris humains traversés d'un battement extraordinaire de ces vers. . . .

The superiority of the ideal drama lies in its revelation of the meaning of human destiny. The awareness of the sense of tragedy inherent in life is for Mallarmé a condition rather than an act, a mode of being rather than a series of events. The inner drama which Mallarmé evokes is perforce a static drama, wherein linear anecdote and physical action are reduced if not altogether eliminated.

The poet's interpretation of *Hamlet* is the most striking illustration of this interiorization of the drama. Shakespeare's play, he declares, in words echoing Victor Hugo's description of his *Théâtre en Liberté*, "*est si bien façonnée selon le seul théâtre de notre esprit*," [33] that it is indifferent to the physical setting and may freely dispense with it. We have seen in Mallarmé's early dramatic attempts the powerful shadow of the melancholy Dane, "*personnage unique d'une tragédie intime et occulte,*" exerting on Mallarmé "*une fascination parente de l'angoisse.*" [34] Hamlet is in fact the only character in the play: "*Son solitaire drame!*" For while Mallarmé admits the presence of secondary characters—Horatio, Laertes, Polonius—they exist only as the background for the central figure and move "*selon une réciprocité symbolique des types entre eux ou relativement à une figure seule.*" [35] Everything in the play pivots around Hamlet and is, indeed, only him. Just as Hamlet is the universal hero, so the conflict in Shakespeare's play constitutes the only subject of dramatic presentation: "*l'antagonisme de rêves chez l'homme avec les fatalités à son existence départies par le malheur.*" [36] In this collision of dream and destiny we have the full expression of the tragedy of the human condition. The subject of *Hamlet* is in this sense universal, independent of accidental or particular circumstances and free from the confines of anecdotal description. This cosmic symbolization may well have its origin in a deep affinity which Mallarmé, like many nineteenth-century poets, saw between himself and Hamlet: "*le spectacle d'un homme s'isolant en lui-même.*" [37] Historically, he declares, the play is a culminating point in the development of a vision of the ideal drama, "*le Monologue ou drame avec Soi, futur.*" [38] In this sense, Shakespeare is the great precursor of the symbolist drama.

Characteristically, Mallarmé finds the same absolute separation between visible and invisible action also present in *Macbeth*. Drawing directly upon the argument of De Quincey in his famous essay, "On the Knocking at the Gate in *Macbeth*," Mallarmé examines the witches' scene, not as part of the action but "*extra-scéniquement,*" as a sudden and violent eruption of fantasy and mystery. The witches are part of the fatality hovering over the play. They do not enter or leave the stage: "*sont là, en tant que le destin qui préexiste*" (349). Their appearance is the overture that leads both to the physical action and to the invisible realm beyond it. Suggestion and incantation dominate the scene. The essay "*La Fausse Entrée des Sorcières dans 'Macbeth'*" is yet another instance of Mallarmé's effort to assimilate Shakespeare into a symbolist theory of drama; it reveals an unusual sensitivity to the magic and wonder of the Shakespearean theater and makes one regret that Mallarmé did not write more essays like it.

Detheatricalization is an important characteristic of the symbolist drama as it came to be developed by Mallarmé's followers and by other playwrights who responded to the symbolist aesthetic. This reduction of the physical attributes of the drama and particularly of the role of artifice and visual effect does not imply a total elimination of the histrionic properties of the art. Mallarmé was fascinated by the spectacle of the empty stage [39] and could claim that reading a play is quite the same as seeing it; [40] nevertheless, he was keenly aware of the attraction of purely theatrical effects and their claims on the attention of the audience. This is not to deny the poet's deep disdain for the fashionable theater of the day. In the last years of his life he seldom went to the theater, out of the conviction that the drama in his day was a debased art. [41] Yet, both in his critical essays and in conversation, Mallarmé demonstrated a keen understanding of the physical theater, of the importance not only of plot action, but also of the set, costumes, and scenic effects as part of the experience of drama. [42] There is a paradox in the poet's preference for the dematerialized stage and the vivid appreciation of its theatrical qualities which may be seen in his spontaneous expression of delight over a performance of *La Vieillesse de Scapin* at the Théâtre Français. [43] It may be that Mallarmé's reduction of décor, gesture, and theatrical artifice was applicable only to the drama of high philosophical purpose and not to the simpler forms of popular entertainment.

In the realm of the ideal theater this paradox is apparent but not troublesome. If we view "*Le Livre*" as an absolute reduction of the play to the book, it is difficult to see how the ceremonial character of the drama would be maintained. [44] Clearly, Mallarmé did not mean to separate the eye and the mind, the spectator and the reader, in any complete sense.

"*Le Livre*" is intended for stage performance as well as for spiritual performance. It is addressed to the masses as well as to the individual. The ideal theater, Mallarmé implies, will fuse aristocratic and popular elements; it will be at once drama for an elite and drama for the public at large. The "*Ode, dramatisée*" is both poem and play. The poet may reduce theatrical elements; he cannot eliminate them. Drama for Mallarmé rises out of an interplay of the book and the theater, that is, out of the exploitation of all of the resources of both the book and the arts of the stage. In this interaction, the purely theatrical is not abandoned; rather, it is placed in a new relationship to all of the elements of dramatic performance.

In Mallarmé's concern with the exploitation of all of the arts in the theater there is a lively awareness of the rich visual and auditory evocation of the ideal made possible by the stage. If the poet never deviated from his conviction that poetry is the highest of the arts, he envisioned the drama as a combination of dance, music, and poetry,[45] along with mime, décor, and indeed all of the arts of the theater. The interrelation of the arts is for Mallarmé part of the essential character of stage performance; it is not a new and separate kind of drama, but an expression of the qualities and capacities that reside within the art of drama itself. In the origin of the drama as well as in its destiny, the arts of the theater are inseparable. At the same time, however, their functions and interrelations are expressed wholly in keeping with their individual properties.

The dance is for Mallarmé the primary and elemental art of the theater, and his reflections on the art of the dance are among the most sensitive and penetrating of his critical speculations.[46] The dance is the source of the poetic character of the theater: the concretion of dream and spirituality, the pure expression of the Idea "*au travers du rite . . . dans la flottaison de rêverie.*"[47] In this sense, the dance is not to be identified with the drama but rather with poetry in the theater. Of all the arts of the theater the dance alone absolutely requires the physical stage, "*un espace réel, ou la scène.*"[48] Drama, the poet implies, can be set forth in a book; the dance cannot. It is for this reason that Mallarmé calls ballet "*la forme théâtrale de poésie par excellence*" (308). No doubt, he would extend this definition to embrace all manifestations of the dance. Mallarmé sometimes seems to use "*Ballet*" and "*Danse*" interchangeably, although on occasion he draws a sharp distinction between them. Ballet is in fact a species of the dance, so that all of the descriptive statements Mallarmé makes about ballet are applicable in a broader sense to the dance as well.

Mallarmé's criticism is at its most poetic in both style and subject in his reflections on the dance. His vision of dance, like that of drama, is altogether nonrepresentational: in its pure and spiritualized expression, the dance does not copy anything. Like Wagner, whose views of the dance the poet criticized, he insists that the "*Ballet, représentable,*" in its literal depiction of reality, does not justify "*le nom de Danse; lequel est, si l'on veut, hiéroglyphe*" (312). The dance, like the drama at large, is assimilated by Mallarmé into a symbolist poetic asserting the primacy of visionary, emblematic, and magical properties of utterance. The poet's theory of the dance implies the same dematerialization of the stage that we have seen in his view of dramatic performance.[49]

Far more completely than the prose drama, the dance is a revelation of our essential attributes and aspirations. Through the infinite suggestiveness of ballet, we may approach "*le paradis de toute spiritualité.*" Whereas the prose drama depends on anecdote, the dance wholly dispenses with it: "*rien n'a lieu, sauf la perfection des exécutants*";[50] while the drama is "*historique,*" the dance is "*emblématique.*" For Mallarmé, narrative and figurative values may exist side by side and may mutually reinforce one another, but in keeping with his principle of purity of genre, he insists that they cannot be freely mixed or dissolved: "*Allier, mais ne confondre.*"[51] Not action but allusion, suggestion, and evocation are the means by which the dance reveals the secret mysteries and hidden analogies of the universe.[52]

The theory of the dance as pure abstraction moves, like Mallarmé's theory of drama, not only toward an art of sug-

94

gestion, but also toward an art of silence.[53] In depersonalizing the dance, the poet sees the dancer as transcending all literal and referential values:

> A savoir que la danseuse *n'est pas une femme qui danse*, pour ces motifs juxtaposés qu'elle *n'est pas une femme*, mais une métaphore résumant un des aspects élémentaires de notre forme, glaive, coupe, fleur, etc., et *qu'elle ne danse pas*, suggérant, par le prodige de raccourcis ou d'élans, avec une écriture corporelle ce qu'il faudrait des paragraphes en prose dialoguée autant que descriptive, pour exprimer, dans la rédaction: poëme dégagé de tout appareil du scribe.[54]

The dancer as metaphor and the dance as poem constitute the purest expression of the ideal that art can yield: poetry liberated from the contingency of language, symbolizing the elemental gestures of our being. The dancer as person gives way to the dancer as the infinitely suggestive image of the ideal, exemplified for Mallarmé by the magic of Loïe Fuller's "*tourbillon de draperies.*" [55] The dance is itself an occasion for reverie and dream, for an apprehension of the mystery of the universe through its "*incorporation visuelle de l'idée*" (306). Herein lies the uniqueness of the dance in the theater, "*seule capable, par son écriture sommaire, de traduire le fugace et le soudain jusqu'à l'Idée*" (541).

Mallarmé's prose-poems on the dance are themselves an evocation of the physical presence of the dancer. If this presence is difficult to seize and impossible to describe or limit, it is nonetheless concrete and visual.[56] Yet, its material expression is but a sign or emblem of its deeper significance. Like the poetic drama, the dance is the celebration of a sacred rite in the temple of the theater.[57] The dancer is not only the plastic representation of the inner life; she is the high priestess in the act of worship in which the performer and the spectator are mutually involved. The mere presence of the dancer serves to hallow and purify the stage, to confer on it "*une virginité de site pas songé*" (308). The reduction or elimination of décor is in full accord with the nudity of the stage on which the dancer, image and symbol, mediate between the finite and the infinite.

The theory of the dance in Mallarmé's aesthetic moves toward the same pure expression of the ideal that we have seen in his theory of "*Le Livre*." As far as we know, Mallarmé planned no choreographic work;[58] he deliberately suppressed the dance in *Hérodiade* out of a preference for the dance as envisioned over the dance as seen.[59] He had no use whatever for the traditional *ballet d'opéra*, which he saw as directly opposed to the evocation of reverie and dream.[60] In its poetic function, the autonomy of the art is absolute. At the same time, precisely because of its total independence of the anecdotal or the literal, the dance in its dramatic context contributes directly to the poetry of the theater. It is the concrete revelation of the ideal, the materialization of silence. Unique among the arts in its magic and spirituality, the dance moves hand in hand with the other arts to bring about a drama of a complex and multiple vision. It is an integral part of the total transformation of the stage.

In his critical writings, Mallarmé gave a new importance to the dance as an art form and, in so doing, called the attention of poets and playwrights of the day to the poetry of the dance in the theater and to the contribution the dance could make in association with the other arts. His reflections are not only a landmark in the theory of the dance; here, more completely than at any other point in his critical writings, they transcend the limitations of the contemporary stage without sacrificing the claims of the physical theater. His observations on the dance served to impel the movement of the drama toward a more intricate and more complex interplay of the arts: toward a poetization of all of the elements of theatrical performance.

The role of music in Mallarmé's theory of drama is based squarely upon his view of the relationship of music to poetry.[61] We have seen that the poet unequivocally rejected Wagner's assertion of the supremacy of music among the arts of the theater. Mallarmé was no less firmly convinced of the intrinsic superiority of poetry to music.[62] Yet, while he accepted the independence of each of the arts in its uniqueness and individuality, he was keenly aware of their dynamic interplay. The musicality of poetry was one of Mallarmé's abiding passions during the latter part of his career. Poetry, he insists, evokes its own music.[63] The separation of poetry and music is for Mallarmé an artificial one: "La Poésie, proche l'idée, est Musique, par excellence—ne consent pas d'infériorité" (381). We must view this bold claim within the context of the long debate with Wagner. Poetry for Mallarmé is not merely an adjunct to music; it is music, just as the reading of poetry is a "*solitaire tacite concert*" (380). We can appreciate the poet's response on learning that Debussy had composed his "*Prélude à l'après-midi d'un Faune*": "Je croyais l'avoir moi-même mis en musique!"[64] In the very act of composition, the poet is perforce a musician. Yet, Mallarmé was opposed to any conception of the music of poetry as mere sound-play.[65] He admonished René Ghil, whose theory of verbal instrumentation he did not share: "Vous phrasez en compositeur, plutôt qu'en écrivain."[66] The music of poetry is not expressed solely in its rhythm, sonority, assonance, or alliteration; these are merely the external signs of the presence of music as an element of the poet's art.

The origin of music for Mallarmé is not orchestral but spiritual: "Toute âme est une mélodie, qu'il s'agit de renouer; et pour cela, sont la flûte ou la viole de chacun" (363). In *La Musique et les Lettres*, Mallarmé varies this formulation only slightly: "*toute âme est un nœud rhythmique*" (644). Music in this sense is the expression of an "*état d'âme*," at one with poetry in its suggestive evocation of mystery. Poetic creation embodies "*la transposition, au Livre, de la symphonie ou uniment de reprendre notre bien*" (367); it is the expression of "*l'ensemble des rapports existant dans tout, la Musique*" (368). Mallarmé's fullest statement of his definition of music was made in a letter of January 10, 1893, to Edmund Gosse, who did not deserve it.[67] Here again, the poet insists that the music of poetry is not external and material; it is "*l'au-delà magiquement produit par certaines dispositions de la parole.*" [68] Mallarmé clarifies his definition as follows:

> . . . c'est la même chose que l'orchestre, sauf que littéraire-ment ou silencieusement. Les poëtes de tous les temps n'ont jamais fait autrement. . . . Employez Musique dans le sens grec, au fond signifiant Idée ou rythme entre des rapports; là, plus divine que dans l'expression publique ou symphonique.

In this sense, music is a necessary part of the structure of poetry: to write poetically is perforce to write musically as well. For Mallarmé, the medium of musical utterance is not ordinary language but rather what he would call the language of silence, the totality of harmonic relationships which constitutes a poem.

Mallarmé's view of the music of poetry applies with equal force to the language of drama. As early as his composition of *Hérodiade* as a tragedy, he sought to make the language of drama issue in the effects of music: "*que toutes ces* impressions *se suivent comme dans une symphonie.*" [69] This deliberate attempt to make poetry in the theater do the work of music gives way, in the later criticism, to a more intimate relation-ship, a response at least in part to the imaginative appeal of Wagner's "total art": "*la Musique rejoint le Vers pour former, depuis Wagner, la Poésie*" (365). In Mallarmé's own writing this interaction is most vividly expressed in the "*mise en scène spirituelle*" of *Un Coup de Dés.*[70] We should not carry the analogy with Wagner too far, but at times, Mallarmé suggests that poetry is akin to the orchestral element of the music-drama and that it occupies the same central role.[71] On the other hand, the residual musicality of the language of poetry is far more important for the poet than any resemblance between this lan-guage and the musical idiom of the Wagnerian opera. As a perceptive critic has observed, for Mallarmé "*le langage con-stitue une sorte de musique transcendante qui conjugue en elle la magie inhérente au monde sonore et la puissance suggestive appartenant au monde spirituel.*" [72] This magic and suggestive-ness belong as fully to the language of the theater as to the

printed page. If the music of silence is rendered most completely in the figure of the mime, the translation of this music
into the ode is uniquely the function of the dramatic poet
(340).[73]

In the theater, music and poetry are both endowed with
"*les moyens réciproques du Mystère*" (649). Mallarmé's liturgical conception of drama draws not only on rhythmic incantation but on the orchestra as well. The ritual celebration of
the mystery of existence takes the form of "*Représentation avec
concert*" (393). Undoubtedly, Mallarmé envisaged instrumental
accompaniment to the dramatic performance. The increased
complexity of stage representation that we have observed in
the poet's view of the dance is evident here as well. Just as the
poetry of the dance is residual rather than extrinsic, so the poetic
drama is intrinsically musical, "*une musicale célébration et
figuration aussi de la vie*" (326). The distinction of "*la
Musique*" and "*les Lettres*" is no more absolute in the theater
than out of it: both are the expression, "*la face alternative*," of
what Mallarmé calls "*l'Idée*" (649). Their appeal is simultane-
ously auditory and visual, literary and theatrical, sensuous and
spiritual. This interaction is implicit in Mallarmé's view of the
centrality of poetry in the theater.

We have observed that Mallarmé's account of the function
of the language of poetry is intimately related to magic and to
the notion of poetry as a revelation of mystery. The reliance
on suggestive evocation through the inherent musicality of language moves poetry toward the plane of silence: "Evoquer,
dans une ombre exprès, l'objet tu, par des mots allusifs, jamais
directs, se réduisant à du silence égal, comporte tentative proche
de créer" (400). This injunction, transferred from the book to
the stage, makes for a theater of mystical suggestiveness and
musicality, in which the resources of the lyric poet come to
be applied to the drama. This exploitation of lyricism and
magic, not only in the language of drama, but also in the
complex configuration of artistic expression, is among the
primary contributions of Mallarmé to the symbolist drama. His

dramatic theory is part of a bold and significant attempt to effect a total reformulation of the art of drama.

It may well be that Mallarmé's image of the theater was mainly theoretical, set forth to be realized by others and never the conscious expression of a goal to be attained by the poet himself.[74] Even so, his dramatic theory is no little achievement. The principles underlying the development of a symbolist drama were stated and elaborated in Mallarmé's critical essays. His concern with language was of central importance, because it was through a new awareness of the function of language in the theater that poetry could regain its rightful place on the stage. If Mallarmé conceived of drama as a "*poème dialogué*," he was also aware of the practical problems confronting the young poet-dramatist: "*il est insupportable d'entendre toujours le même vers pendant cinq actes*," he declared;[75] for, while the classical drama imposed respect and attention, the modern playwright who merely imitated the idiom of Corneille or Racine would run the risk of losing his audience. In the face of the rigidity of the conventions of prose realism and the incompatibility between the poet and the age, Mallarmé had no assurance that his vision of an ideal theater would find expression. He insists that there are elements of the theater of musicality, magic, and dream implanted within the old melodrama, but for the most part the development of a popular theater and a mass audience has taken place "*sans préparer de circonstances neuves ou le milieu mental identifiant la scène et la salle.*" [76] The absence of any principle or controlling idea that might lend direction and order to "*l'engrenage théâtral*" is proof of the impossibility of any rapid amelioration of the low estate of the drama. Nevertheless, Mallarmé does not urge the young poets of the day to flee from the theater, but rather to devote themselves to its reconstruction.[77] The development of the symbolist drama, in France and throughout the whole of Europe, is the direct result of the response of the young poets of the turn of the last century to Mallarmé's appeal.

V

THE EARLY SYMBOLIST DRAMA

FROM MALLARMÉ'S PROGRAMMATIC EFFORTS of the 1880's to the emergence of a symbolist drama in the 1890's, first in France and then throughout Europe, is but a short step. The poet did not live to see fulfillment of his dream of a new poetic theater, but the application of symbolist poetics to the art of the stage, essentially the result of his efforts, began several years before Mallarmé's death. The starting point of symbolist dramatic theory is Mallarmé's series of chronicles in the *Revue Indépendante* in 1886 and 1887; the impact of these essays on the young poets and aspiring playwrights who read and contributed to the review was direct and immediate. Mallarmé reprinted several of the more important articles, with accompanying titles such as "Hamlet" and "Ballets," in *Pages*, published in Brussels in 1891.[1] Subsequent reprintings, notably in the section of *Divagations* in 1897 entitled "Crayonné au Théâtre," served to give wider currency to the poet's vision of an ideal theater. Along with the continual flow of essays during the 1890's, we must also take into account the constant discussion of the theater's ways and means that took place at many of Mallarmé's Tuesday evening gatherings. The preoccupations of the critical essays of 1886-87: Wagner, Hamlet, the dance, the language of drama, the interrelations of the arts, were all constant topics of conversation between the poet and his young admirers. It is impossible to separate the influence of the man from that of his thought. The steady increase in the popularity of the poet brought new attention to his early dramatic compositions as well as to his dramatic theories.[2] Mallarmé's writings were the starting point for the efforts of many new poets and playwrights to transform the theater of the day.

Nevertheless, it would be incorrect to attribute the symbolist venture in the theater exclusively to the author of *Hérodiade*. The impact of Mallarmé's dramatic theory coincides with a number of parallel events: the recognition of the talent of Villiers de l'Isle-Adam; the rediscovery of the theater of Alfred de Musset and of the values of fantasy and imaginative improvisation; the ever-widening diffusion of Wagner's view of the art work of the future; the deliberate efforts of young symbolists to extend the gains of poetry to all of the literary arts; as well as the large share of accident in the emergence of talented playwrights capable of drawing upon Mallarmé's legacy. The restrictions of realistic and naturalistic dramaturgy further served to stimulate experimentation in language, scenic effects, and techniques of symbolization. In his historical setting, Mallarmé is a powerful influence, but he is only one of several forces shaping the emergence of a symbolist drama. Our isolation of the poet's role may suggest that he was uniquely responsible for the course of the new drama, and this is plainly not the case. On the other hand, without Mallarmé the ideals of symbolist drama as well as their concrete realization would not have been the same. Indeed, were it not for the theory and technique set forth in Mallarmé's writings, it is doubtful that we could speak of a symbolist drama at all, any more than of a symbolist poetry.

It would be well to summarize the salient characteristics of symbolist drama as they emerge from Mallarmé's aesthetic:

1. Drama is the expression of inner life, the revelation of an " *état d'âme*."

2. Drama is the expression of mystery: the revelation of the hidden wonder of the universe.

3. The language of drama is poetry rather than prose, evocative rather than descriptive, and relying upon suggestion as opposed to statement.

4. The stage is detheatricalized, reduced to the barest and simplest elements of histrionic performance.

5. The theater brings into play all of the arts, interrelated within a poetic structure.

Not every one of Mallarmé's followers accepted all of these tenets and, in practice, the implementation of symbolist theories was to vary considerably from one playwright to another. It is clear, however, that the programmatic demands for a reorientation of the theater that we find in France in the late 1880's and in the following decade are essentially a restatement of the values of Mallarmé's poetics and his dramatic theory.

No single volume corresponded more closely to a symbolist manifesto than *La Littérature de tout à l'heure* of Charles Morice, published in 1889. We can see Mallarmé's influence directly at work in Morice's view of the future of the drama. The young critic takes due account of Wagner's effort at "*l'union de toutes les formes artistiques,*" [3] but he has serious reservations concerning the dominance of music over poetry. Morice is painfully aware of the gulf separating the theater of the day from what it might become, and if he views the present-day stage as vulgar, profane, and inaccessible to the artist,[4] his vision of the theater as "*fête suprême et synthèse de l'Art et de tous les Arts*" is fully in keeping with Mallarmé's ideal.[5]

Subsequent theoreticians were more interested than Morice in ways in which symbolist poetics might transform the theater. Gustave Kahn, in a programmatic essay of 1889, insisted that the theater constituted "*la grande forme d'art,*" capable of multiple and varied interpretations.[6] His plea is for a poetic conception of the theater, in accord with "*notre tissu mélodique de phrases et la position plastique de nos pensées.*" [7] Kahn envisions a theater of "*milieu indéfini,*" embracing pantomime and ballet, and drawing upon popular as well as literary modes of theatrical expression. Mallarmé himself would not have put it differently. Other essays of the early 1890's lent further support to the idea of a symbolist drama, a theater founded on the premise of multiple interpretations: "*que chaque mystère découvert fût l'enveloppe d'un mystère toujours plus ténébreux offert à des intuitions toujours plus pénétrantes."* [8] Camille Mauclair in the *Revue Indépendante* for March 1892 demanded the restoration of the poet in the theater and envisaged *" une langue magnifique où la poésie resplendira."* [9] Pierre Valin sought to reconcile the interrelations of the arts with the principle of *correspondances* in the theater: *" harmoniser toutes choses: décors, faits, sentiments, paroles, types, de manière à obtenir sur le public la sensation la plus correspondante à l'état d'âme de l'acteur principal."* [10] Particularly as a repertoire of symbolist drama began to emerge, critics, playwrights, and producers sought to give meaning and direction to the new tendencies; they did so largely by returning to the principles of dramatic expression set forth by Mallarmé. As Remy de Gourmont was to declare, *" le programme d'un drame ésotérique, tout en allusions à la vie, où les idées seraient* suggérées *et non* exprimées" represents *" la pure doctrine de Mallarmé."* [11]

The vigor of Mallarmé's aesthetic in the literature of the 1890's is in large measure the consequence of his role as guide and counselor to the young writers of the day.[12] Warm, sympathetic to the point of fault, eager to help young poets learn their craft, he epitomized the idea of the poet for the writers of his time. The *Album* offered to Mallarmé by his disciples and friends in March 1897 provides in its table of contributors a list of the principal symbolist poets and playwrights in France: Claudel, Gide, Maeterlinck, Régnier, Vielé-Griffin, Rodenbach, Valéry, Verhaeren, and several others.[13] The symbolist movement in both theory and expression was a tribute to the triumph of Mallarmé's art as the principal source of *" le goût du mystère, du vague, du délicieux imprécis"* in the new literature of the day.[14] As early as 1887, Emile Verhaeren could state, "A cette heure, il n'est qu'un vrai maître symboliste en France: Stéphane Mallarmé." [15] With the passage of time, Mallarmé has become even more fully identified with the symbolist movement.

If we may see the groundwork of a symbolist drama in Mallarmé's dramatic projects and especially in his theoretical writings, the existence of a symbolist drama in the theater is the result of the efforts of a younger generation of writers who were more naturally inclined toward theatrical expression than was the author of *Hérodiade*. Thibaudet has described Mallarmé's vision of the theater as enveloped in a "*nuage de possibilité*."[16] It required the talents of Vielé-Griffin, Van Lerberghe, Maeterlinck, Claudel, Régnier, Verhaeren, and their confreres to make the poet's ideals take on actuality. As early as 1890, Adolphe Retté could assert the existence of a symbolist drama: [17]

> Désormais, la preuve est faite: il y a un théâtre symboliste; deux drames sont à l'actif du groupe: *Ancaeus, La Princesse Maleine*. Il s'en présentera d'autres.

And in fact, other plays were not long in coming. Paul Fort's Théâtre d'Art was established in 1890 as part of a deliberate attempt to open the way to "*une littérature dramatique symboliste*."[18] The absorption of its impulses soon afterwards in the Théâtre de l'Œuvre provided the new symbolist drama with a sympathetic, if restricted, public and with the practical means of working toward the transformation of the theater.

The establishment and role of Lugné-Poe's Théâtre de l'Œuvre as the temple of symbolist drama has been ably and comprehensively described by Jacques Robichez, and repetition would be superfluous. However, it would be well for us, in passing, to keep in mind the close personal as well as theoretical relationships between Lugné-Poe and Mallarmé. The conception of the Théâtre de l'Œuvre, its founder declared, was of a theater wherein "*l'Idée reste supérieure et intacte*."[19] Lugné-Poe's ideal of a theater "*où s'associeraient poésie et silences*"[20] reflects his deep spiritual kinship with Mallarmé. In his concern with a décor of suggestiveness and atmospheric evocation, he shared the poet's conviction that theatrical devices should be effaced, subdued, if not entirely eliminated. The reduction of décor, absence of movement, monotonous manner of speech, and low emotional pressure, characteristic of Lugné-Poe's productions of Ibsen as well as of Maeterlinck, represent the counterpart of Mallarmé's plea for detheatricalization.[21] In his memoirs, Lugné-Poe tells of talks with the poet, evidently in the summer of 1893, in which Mallarmé elaborated a plan for a theater of open-air performances, reminiscent of the Théâtre de Valvins: [22]

> Il aimait parler théâtre. Je me souviens que, se promenant sur la rive, il se laissa aller jusqu'à inventer un théâtre qui aurait donné ses spectacles en plein air, pendant l'été. La scène eût été le rivage, champ—orée d'un bois,—ferme, etc., tandis que les spectateurs seraient assis sur une sorte de chaland. La salle seule eût été mobile, et ainsi le théâtre se serait déplacé selon le caprice du directeur.

The open-air theater is not merely one way in which Mallarmé sought to obliterate the restrictions of the physical stage; it points unmistakably to a return to the simple and elemental conditions of performance so as to make of the theater a lay ritual, akin to the festive ceremony of the drama of ancient Greece. It is a theater wholly in keeping with the drama of Banville or of the *Faune* "Intermède." The appeal to the imaginative powers of the director must have especially attracted Lugné-Poe. The open-air theater did not originate with the symbolists, nor was it sufficiently developed by them. Nevertheless, it provides another fine example of the bold experimental attitude of Mallarmé and his followers toward the drama.

The idea of an open-air theater was dear to Lugné-Poe. In all likelihood, it was he who directed the performance of Henri de Régnier's *La Gardienne* at Presles, at the edge of the forest of l'Isle-Adam, "*sur un théâtre naturel creusé dans la montagne.*" [23] The simplicity and purity of the outdoor theater— which Lugné-Poe studied with particular interest in the English drama of the late Middle Ages—contrast sharply with the modern stage, wherein everything conspires to destroy the "*sentiment du* mystère." [24] Like Mallarmé, he preferred the stage empty: "*Pas de décor ou peu*"; [25] and in this radical simplification he saw a means whereby poetry could recover its purity and centrality in dramatic performance.

Lugné-Poe hailed the reduction of theatrical artifice in the drama of Maurice Maeterlinck as a sign of "*l'éclosion d'une nouvelle forme dramatique.*" [26] In retrospect we may see the intrinsic and historical limitations of Maeterlinck's drama, and even Mallarmé, as we shall observe, did not fully share Lugné-Poe's enthusiastic appreciation. Nevertheless, on the plane of achieved dramatic composition, it is fair to assert that Maeterlinck constitutes the "*représentant quasi officiel de l'apport des Symbolistes au théâtre.*" [27] This is not the place for a detailed consideration of the scope and limits of Maeterlinck's art and its significance in the modern theater, but his relationship to Mallarmé is central to any discussion of the poet's role in the development of symbolist drama.

Maeterlinck can be described as a symbolist playwright not only because of his close personal relations with the leaders of the movement in Paris, but also because his literary aims and values are a consequence of his deep familiarity with the broad tradition of symbolist theory and expression. Not only Villiers and Mallarmé, but also Swedenborg and Novalis, Carlyle and Emerson, Poe and Baudelaire, Verlaine and Laforgue, all contributed to the formation of Maeterlinck's symbolist view of life and art.[28] In Paris in 1886 the young Flemish lawyer came under the spell of Villiers, whose reading of the newly composed sections of *Axël* impressed him profoundly.[29] Even at the beginning of his career, Maeterlinck declared, with mingled truth and exaggeration: "Tout ce que j'ai fait, c'est à Villiers que je le dois, à ses conversations plus qu'à ses œuvres que j'admire beaucoup d'ailleurs." [30] On his return to Ghent it was, no doubt, mainly due to Villiers' inspiration that Maeterlinck resolved to become a writer.[31] Yet, in Maeterlinck's art the impact of Villiers cannot be readily distinguished from the influence of all the other contributors to the symbolist movement. With Mallarmé as with Villiers, the Belgian playwright shares a common set of attitudes and values that are themselves the fruit of a long poetic tradition. These traditional elements were translated into a dramatic technique that is in close accord with Mallarmé's vision of theatrical performance. There can be no doubt that Maeterlinck was familiar with Mallarmé's work and learned from it; nevertheless, the relationship is far more one of affinity than one of influence, and it is expressed not only in a common derivation from a pervasive symbolist heritage, but also in the immediate literary and theatrical affiliations of the young Belgian playwright.

The one-act play of Charles Van Lerberghe, *Les Flaireurs* (1889), is a landmark in the symbolist drama; its importance within the broader panorama of the modern theater has seldom been adequately appreciated.[32] This is not the place for a detailed consideration of Van Lerberghe's powerful evocation of mystery and terror. He wrote the play, he declared, "*suivant le procédé indiqué par Poe dans la genèse d'un poème en prenant pour base l'effet de terreur d'un frappement à la porte.*"[33] The drama of suggestion and dread expectation, wherein the spiritual and material realms interact and in which the presence of death dominates the atmosphere, clearly anticipates such plays of Maeterlinck as *L'Intruse* and *Les Aveugles*. Albert Mockel hailed *Les Flaireurs* as a noteworthy innovation in the drama, a play wherein "*on écoute chanter en soi l'idéal orchestre qu'on rêve,*"[34] fully in keeping with the dramatic ideals of Mallarmé. In his programmatic utterances Mockel pointed directly toward the plays of Maeterlinck and the rise of a symbolist drama, a drama that "would use music and poetry to create rhythmic continuity, and legendary subjects to create esthetic distance."[35]

Maeterlinck's debt to Van Lerberghe is real, even if it was somewhat exaggerated by the author of *L'Intruse* in his early career. In a letter of 1892 attached to the program for a performance of *Les Flaireurs*, Maeterlinck leaves no doubt about Van Lerberghe's priority in technique, and he even declares that *Les Flaireurs* possesses "*une puissance de symbolisation*" that *L'Intruse* lacks.[36] The futile attempt to appease the invisible in the face of "*l'invasion des ténèbres sans fin*" is for Maeterlinck the principal source of the theme and structure of his own plays. On the other hand, Van Lerberghe pointed out, shortly after the composition of his play, that he had made certain alterations according to suggestions of Maeterlinck.[37] Without impugning Van Lerberghe's originality, it would seem that

Maeterlinck's personal influence and the genuine rapport between the two friends make it difficult to establish any sharp
separation in priority or technique in their early literary efforts.

At the time of the composition of *Les Flaireurs*, Van
Lerberghe's admiration for Mallarmé was passionate and sustained.[38] With due allowance for his later rejection of symbolist poetics, as far as the late 1880's it is accurate to hold that
" Mallarmé n'eut pas de disciple plus convaincu." [39] This fervent
admiration was shared by Maeterlinck. In an entry in his
Journal in 1889, Van Lerberghe declared that the discovery of
Mallarmé constituted, for both Maeterlinck and himself, a
literary revolution: [40]

> Les anciens dieux furent renversés de leur pinacle sauf
> Baudelaire. J'appris Mallarmé par coeur, je le déclamai du
> haut de mon balcon, je le chantai dans les allées de mon
> jardin. Le Faune avait été rapporté de Paris par Maeter-
> linck. Ce fut lui aussi qui apporta un soir au grand café dans
> une gazette la splendide Hérodiade. Ah! l'écarquillement
> de nos yeux éblouis devant ce miracle à cette petite table
> du grand café solitaire.

Van Lerberghe goes on to state, in his journal, "*pour Maeterlinck et moi le dieu de la Poésie nouvelle devint Mallarmé,*" and
he adds: "L'influence de Mallarmé fut incontestable sur nous,
sur moi surtout." [41] Also in 1889, he visited Paris and met Mallarmé; clearly, the French poet exerted the same profound personal impact on the young Belgians as he did on most of the
young French poets and playwrights of his time. Not only
Mallarmé's poetry, but also his dramatic compositions and his
critical essays captivated Van Lerberghe and Maeterlinck at the
very beginning of their careers. The efforts of the young Belgians to create a symbolist drama are a direct response to
Mallarmé's endeavor.

There is yet nearer proof of the spiritual and personal
attachment of Maeterlinck and Mallarmé. The young Belgian's
collection of poems, *Serres Chaudes* (1889), is a representative
volume of the epoch in its misty evocation of analogies and

symbols in an idiom alternatingly suggesting Verlaine and Mallarmé. With sympathetic penetration, Verhaeren viewed Maeterlinck's lyrics as typically symbolist poems, "*qui planent sur le pays vague, mystérieux et séducteur*," reflecting the meditations of the poet "*très loin dans l'isolement du rêve.*" [42] Even more plainly than in his poetry, the impact of symbolist theories and techniques is evident in Maeterlinck's early critical statements. In a programmatic essay of 1890, Maeterlinck complained of the disappearance of "*la densité mystique de l'œuvre d'art*" and of the conception of the theater as "*le temple du rêve.*" [43] He, like Mallarmé, shares Charles Lamb's conviction that the plays of Shakespeare are unfit for stage performance. The young Belgian insists that the greatest dramatic compositions are addressed to the inner theater of the mind, wherein their symbolic value is not destroyed by the accidents of physical performance. The new theater will turn away from anecdote and individual experience to a drama wherein the human figure may come to be replaced "*par une ombre, un reflet, une projection de formes symboliques.* . . ." [44] The same symbolist values are restated and amplified in the interview of 1891 with Jules Huret. By this time Maeterlinck was acquiring fame as a playwright; yet his remarks, more general than in the essay of 1890, could apply with equal force to poetry as well. Like his counterparts in France, the young Belgian is not interested in reportage or in documentary realism, but rather in freeing himself from "*des contingences de l'actualité immédiate.*" [45] The power of the poet rises not from himself but from what he accomplishes "*par les autres, et par l'ordre mystérieux et éternel et la force occulte des choses.*" [46] Like Dujardin, Wyzewa, Mauclair, and the other young poets and critics who grouped themselves around Mallarmé, Maeterlinck considered the symbol intrinsic to all poetic expression: "*s'il n'y a pas de symbole, il n'y a pas d'œuvre d'art.*" His reflections on the nature of symbolic expression are not in any fundamental way to be distinguished from contemporary discussions of symbolist aesthetics. It is characteristic of Maeterlinck, however, that for him symbols are to be found in the simplest manifestations of common life, rather than in abstractions which a poet may seek to impose on reality. More familiar than most of his French contemporaries with the symbolist aesthetics of German Romanticism, Maeterlinck could draw on Goethe's distinction between allegory and symbol as a way of distinguishing between purely local and universal symbolic values in literature. Yet, unlike Goethe but very much in the manner of Mallarmé and his contemporaries, Maeterlinck fused his symbolist view of poetry with the occult and mystical interpretation of the universe underlying the poetics of *correspondances*.

Mallarmé's personal role in Maeterlinck's career was of immense and indeed crucial importance.[47] It should be recalled that, despite a few scattered notices of his early work, as far as the French public was concerned Maeterlinck was practically an unknown writer until the publication of the article by Octave Mirbeau on *La Princesse Maleine* in *Le Figaro* for August 24, 1890.[48] Few beginnings have been subject to such lavish praise. For Mirbeau, *La Princesse Maleine* was the greatest masterpiece of the modern drama, "*supérieure en beauté à ce qu'il y a de plus beau dans Shakespeare.*" The effects were extraordinary, in the bookshops as well as in the theater: Maeterlinck was launched on his public career. Only later did it become clear that Mirbeau—who did not know Maeterlinck personally—had written his famous article at the behest of Mallarmé.[49] As the playwright himself declared in his memoirs written near the end of his life, "*c'était Stéphane Mallarmé qui, angéliquement confraternel, lui avait communiqué l'exemplaire qu'il avait reçu, en appelant sur mon œuvre la vigilante attention du grand polémiste.*"[50] This act of generosity was typical of Mallarmé's concern for the interest and welfare of the young poets and playwrights who drew upon his precept and example, transforming his ideals into a new mode of literary expression. We have seen from the remarks of Van Lerberghe that Maeterlinck's appreciation of Mallarmé antedated by several months the intercession of the French poet on his behalf. In a letter of August 3, 1890—three weeks before the appearance of Mirbeau's article—Maeterlinck confided to Albert Mockel that he ranked Mallarmé higher than Verlaine because of the loftiness of Mallarmé's aspirations.[51] Some years later Mockel requested a contribution from Maeterlinck for the collective *Album* of March 1897; while the dramatist's reply expresses some hesitation, this is not, he insists, because of any lack of sympathy and appreciation on his part: "Il y a peu d'hommes au monde que j'admire et que j'aime autant que Mallarmé."[52] In the same vein, Maeterlinck attested to his genuine admiration for the poet in describing Mallarmé as "*un des plus grands penseurs et des plus hauts esprits de ce monde.*"[53] These spontaneous and scattered expressions do not in themselves suggest any close relationship; yet when we examine Maeterlinck's plays in relation to Mallarmé's dramatic theory, we shall find further evidence of a deep and pervasive affinity that links the two writers to a common enterprise in the modern theater.

The description and elaboration of Mallarmé's ideal drama constitute a direct anticipation of the plays of Maeterlinck. Indeed, Mallarmé's reduction of narrative would make for an even more thoroughgoing static drama than we can find anywhere in Maeterlinck. The language of allusion and suggestion, dream and mystery, in drama as well as in poetry, is fundamental to Mallarmé's vision of art. This mistiness and complex atmospheric evocation are present, he insists, in popular theatrical forms as well as in more intimate and more literary dramatic compositions; Mallarmé's conception of the old popular melodrama is a striking anticipation of Maeterlinck's theater.[54] If this theater culminates in a drama of silence or at any rate in an evocation of the interpenetration of speech and silence, this suggestiveness too is wholly in accord with symbolist poetics. In a letter to Georges Rodenbach in 1888, Mallarmé declared: "*cet art consiste, n'est-ce pas? le suprême, à ne jamais en les chantant, dépouiller des objets, subtils et regardés, du voile justement de Silence sous quoi ils nous séduisirent et transparaît maintenant le Secret de leur Signification.*"[55] This description of the essence of poetry could also be read as an account of the language of Maeterlinck's drama and the effect of this drama on its audience.

A detailed examination of Maeterlinck's plays would carry us well beyond the limits of our study; nevertheless, it would be valuable for us to perceive more nearly how his plays reflect the dramatic aims and values of Mallarmé. All of Maeterlinck's early dramas: *La Princesse Maleine, L'Intruse, Les Aveugles,* and *Les Sept Princesses,* portray essentially passive characters subject to the overpowering pressures of hidden, mysterious forces. Space and time are narrowly confined; yet the boundaries of the plane of action are fluid rather than fixed, losing clarity and even identity in their interaction with the shadowy realm of the infinite. The narrative in Maeterlinck's first play, *La Princesse Maleine* (1889), is marked by all the violence and physically induced horror of Romantic tragedy, but the action is constantly retarded by means of repetition of words or phrases, elongation of scenes, elaboration of atmospheric effects, and other devices that serve mainly to intensify the feeling of mystery and horror.[56] The play is built around the helplessness of pure innocence in the face of absolute evil. Maeterlinck does not wholly suspend the traditional linear plot; rather, he distends it, thereby reducing its importance. The broad symbolization of experience in the drama endeared the play to Mallarmé and his followers. Albert Mockel viewed *La Princesse Maleine* as an incarnation of "*ce théâtre où tendent nos désirs, le théâtre où parmi les magies d'éclatants ou lointains décors un acte se dresse, que l'on sait totale.*"[57] For Mockel, as for many of Mallarmé's adherents, Maeterlinck's drama represented a conception of theater as a "*réalisation plastique d'un poème*"; a cosmic drama much as Mallarmé himself had attempted and defined: not the representation of "une *anecdote et* un *individu,*" but rather "*l'histoire éternelle de l'Homme.*"[58] Maeterlinck did not wholly suppress the anecdotal and individual, but his drama moves in this direction. As we may see in other symbolist plays as well, the drama of purely individual experience is at sharp variance with the new aspiration toward infinite suggestiveness.

The interpenetration of physical and spiritual planes of existence which Maeterlinck derived from occult and symbolist tradition finds expression not only in atmospheric devices reminiscent of the Gothic, but also in strident and frenzied emotion that contrasts violently on the stage with the static dramatic action. In *Les Sept Princesses*, the intensity of feeling rises from the juxtaposition of the Queen's passion to the eery suggestiveness and silence, pointing to the presence of invisible and hostile forces. This evocation of mystery is the translation into dramatic terms of the same poetics of *correspondances* which dominates Mallarmé's vision of the theater and, indeed, all of his literary endeavors.

Mallarmé's appreciation of Maeterlinck's art was genuine and profound. In the second of two theater chronicles composed for the *National Observer* (London) in June 1893, he defined the significance of the young Belgian's drama in relation to the emerging patterns of symbolist drama in France. The new playwrights conceive of the theater as the expression of "*la scène intérieure*," wherein "*Un ensemble versifié convie à une idéale représentation*," a theater of dream and spirituality free from the restrictions of the actual. Maeterlinck is part of this poetic current of the modern stage. The young French poets who share Mallarmé's vision of the theater, Vielé-Griffin, Régnier, and others, have constructed their plays by providing "*par la convergence de fragments harmoniques à un centre, là même, une source de drame latente qui reflue à travers le poëme*" (329). Maeterlinck shares their effort to restore the theater to its larger poetic context; like the French playwrights, Maeterlinck "*inséra le théâtre au livre!*" (329). All the same, there is an essential difference in dramatic structure: whereas the French poets have attempted a fusion of poetic and operatic values in a complex symphonic pattern, Maeterlinck has turned wholly away from the Wagnerian "*polyphonie magnifique instrumentale*" to a pattern of sequential action "*avec une expresse succession de scènes, à la Shakespeare*." In this respect, Maeterlinck's art is far more traditional in its literary affiliations.

Nevertheless, Mallarmé does not share the easy identification of Maeterlinck and the author of *Hamlet* and *King Lear*.[59] The young playwright's salient qualities are uniquely his own, for while Shakespeare's characters *"agissent en toute vie, tangibles, . . . corporels,"* those of Maeterlinck are vague, shadowy, phantasmagoric (329). The stage setting itself constitutes *"un massif arrêt de toute réalité,"* devoid of any sense of concrete or literal representation: *"on est loin, par ces fantômes, de Shakespeare"* (330).

This is not to say that, for Mallarmé, Maeterlinck's drama is lacking in theatrical effectiveness. The simplicity of action and the striking atmospheric evocation of mystery and dread in *Pelléas et Mélisande* constitute for Mallarmé *"une variation supérieure sur l'admirable vieux mélodrame"* (330). If we recall the poet's earlier dramatic projects, we may view his appraisal of the rudimentary and popular elements of Maeterlinck's art as praise, not blame. Furthermore, in speaking of *"une variation supérieure,"* Mallarmé alludes not merely to the superiority of the young playwright's dramatic technique, but to the *"essence supérieure"* of the theater itself—a spiritual evocation of the mystery of existence. Mallarmé views *Pelléas et Mélisande* as an indication of but one of many ways in which a theater *"de vision et de songes"* may find expression, and clearly it is not held forth as the sole model for other symbolist playwrights; nevertheless, there can be no doubt that for Mallarmé this play, along with Maeterlinck's earlier dramas, represents a significant achievement in the modern theater.

It is again through contrast with Wagner that this significance is made clear. In sharp opposition to the composer's subordination of poetry to music, Maeterlinck's drama dispenses with instrumentation by providing its own music: *"Silencieusement presque et abstraitement au point que dans cet art, où tout devient musique dans le sens propre, la partie d'un instrument même pensif, violon, nuirait, par inutilité"* (330). In this sense, the atmosphere of Maeterlinck's theater of magic is suffused with music; it is a living demonstration of the power of the poet in the theater, and the *"authenticité de son intime munificence."* For Mallarmé, Maeterlinck's drama was a poetic drama in the fullest sense, *"un Drame . . . réglé par les conflits mélodiques"* (861), wherein poetry constitutes its own music.

Maeterlinck's subsequent career was to justify Mallarmé's belief that suspense and dramatic tension were important elements of the art of the Belgian playwright. The increasingly overt exploitation of the resources of Romantic melodrama in Maeterlinck's later work represents a deliberate rejection of the symbolist values of his early dramatic theory and technique, but it is not in his later work that his importance resides. Mallarmé saw Maeterlinck's theater in the early 1890's as part of an attempt to restore magnificence and wonder to the stage through the evocation of inner life. In this effort, the Belgian playwright joins hands with his symbolist precursors and notably with Mallarmé, whose aesthetics of the theater he shared and embodied in his work. Within the larger framework of symbolist drama, Maeterlinck is not as lyrical as Hofmannsthal nor as intense as Yeats, but his plays served as the principal source of the diffusion of symbolist theories and techniques in the modern European theater. Maeterlinck's early work is to this day important for its exploration of new possibilities of dramatic expression. With all allowance made for the undeniable talent of the playwright, what is new in Maeterlinck is his assimilation of symbolist values within a traditional dramatic setting. His early career provides yet further proof of the rich imaginative and experimental character of the legacy of Mallarmé and his followers in the theater.

The inspiration and guidance which Mallarmé provided for the Belgian poets and playwrights was for the most part indirect and in association with other currents and forces in the symbolist tradition. We should not ignore the role of Mallarmé himself as an intermediary. The poet's lecture in Belgium in February 1890 on Villiers de l'Isle-Adam revealed *Axël* and its symbolist dramaturgy to many young Belgian writers.[60] Nonetheless, Mallarmé's role in the shaping of the new drama was largely immediate and personal, particularly in Paris where he gave constant and sympathetic encouragement to young writers in whom he discovered a talent for the theater.

Along with such Belgian followers as Verhaeren, Rodenbach, Van Lerberghe, and Maeterlinck, Mallarmé provided direction and support for many young French admirers and disciples: Vielé-Griffin, Claudel, Régnier, Jammes, Gide, Saint-Pol-Roux, Valéry, and countless others who sought to bring about a symbolist drama. It is impossible to isolate Mallarmé's contribution from the development of the symbolist drama; in a few brief pages we can consider only a few illustrations of the poet's impact on his young contemporaries and the significance of their common enterprise.

As we observed in our discussion of Mallarmé and Wagner, the aims of the composer and the poet were at least superficially identical: both sought to bring together poetry and music, and both relied on suggestiveness and mystery as essential sources of dramatic effect. In spite of the very real separation between Wagner and the poets of the theater of the 1890's, Wagner's theories and techniques were often conjoined with those of Mallarmé in the works of the younger symbolists. A striking example is provided by Francis Vielé-Griffin's first full-length play, *Ancaeus* (1888), one of the earliest symbolist dramas.[61] Rich in atmospheric effects and in the lyrical celebration of love, the play is a reworking of characters and events from Greek mythology. Song and choric chant lend support to the markedly operatic climax. The drinking of the love philter and the death of Ancaeus following the passionate embrace of his beloved point unmistakably to the finale of Wagner's *Tristan* or to Villiers' *Axël*. Mallarmé does not seem to have been impressed by the melodramatic effects of *Ancaeus;* yet he had high praise for the poet's attempt to fuse poetry and the drama: " *comme tant qu'il n'y aura pas un théâtre pour les pompes secrètes, outre la Musique, je crois qu'il faut s'en tenir au genre par vous excellemment rénoué.*" [62] Vielé-Griffin's last play, *Phocas le jardinier*, probably represents his closest approximation to Mallarmé's ideal. Here, while the narrative comes sharply to the fore in the conflict of pagan and Christian, the emphasis is on the inner struggle of Phocas and on the revelation of his " *état d'âme.*" Without subscribing to the view that *Phocas le jardinier* is the loftiest French drama since Racine,[63] we may see in the play a deliberate effort to reconcile the claims of lyric and dramatic poetry. Vielé-Griffin's plays, like most late symbolist dramas, were neglected by the Théâtre de l'Œuvre;[64] today, their interest is exclusively historical, as further evidence of the mysticism and spirituality characteristic of the young poets of the end of the last century.

The early literary career of Paul Claudel offers another instance of Mallarmé's understanding and encouragement of young writers at a decisive moment in their development. The opposition to Mallarmé in Claudel's later work is profound,[65] and it plainly would not do to see his drama as merely another manifestation of symbolist endeavor. On the other hand, Claudel's indebtedness to Mallarmé was immense, not only during his years of apprenticeship, but also throughout his literary career.[66] The relationship is complex and we cannot hope to examine it here in full detail. From 1887 to 1895, Claudel visited Mallarmé, participating in the "*mardis*," exchanging letters and publications with the older poet, and acquiring through him an initiation into the mysteries of the poetic art. To be sure, Claudel had certain reservations from the very beginning of his friendship with Mallarmé. In an entry in his *Journal* in March 1889, Romain Rolland declared of the young Claudel: "*il est du cénacle de Mallarmé et de Villiers de l'Isle-Adam, mais il dit franchement qu'il ne les admire que pour la forme; il fait bon marché de leur métaphysique.*"[67] There is a large element of truth in this account, even after due allowance is made for Rolland's hostility to Mallarmé and to his "*adeptes assez médiocres.*"[68] At the same time, other sources assure us that Claudel acquired more from Mallarmé than the mechanical processes of composition. In a letter of 1930, Claudel declared that in order to study his work one should first understand the atmosphere of the 1880's in which he developed, and especially the dominance of Mallarmé. A sympathetic reader of Claudel has declared, "*les propos qu'il entendait chez Mallarmé sont ceux-là même que nous retrouverons sous sa plume tout au long de sa vie.*"[69] For Claudel, as for all the young writers of his generation, the teaching and example of Mallarmé were decisive forces in his career.

It was Mallarmé more than any other single writer who provided Claudel with a definition of the relationship of the poet to his art. As he later declared, Mallarmé was for him an admirable "*professeur d'attention.*" [70] The meaning of language, the importance of clarity and precision in the use of words, the dignity and grandeur of the poet's calling, all were part of the lesson taught by Mallarmé. We may see the homage of a disciple to his master in Claudel's letter to Mallarmé of March 25, 1895 wherein he declares: "Nul esprit plus que vous n'était fondé à revendiquer le haut droit des Lettres dans lesquelles vous exercez la magistrature: l'intelligence." The conclusion of the letter, even while implying a certain distance, leaves no doubt of the young poet's attitude: "Laissez-moi . . . me féliciter de la fortune que j'ai eue de rencontrer au début de ma carrière littéraire votre conversation, votre exemple et votre amitié." [71] Not only the man but his ideals and aspirations as well made a profound mark on the young poet. The notion of poetry as a mysterious revelation of the hidden wonder of the universe, the *correspondance* between the visible and invisible planes of reality, the suggestive and evocative power of language, all enter directly into Claudel's poetic vision. If he soon separated himself sharply from what he considered the spiritual emptiness and nihilism of Mallarmé's philosophical values, he did not abandon the symbolist aesthetic, but rather incorporated it into his religious convictions. [72] Despite his subsequent refusals to admit it, Claudel's debt to his "*milieu littéraire symboliste et mallarméen*" is immense. [73] Even after many expressions of deep separation, late in life Claudel could still allude to Mallarmé as "*mon vieux maître*" and to "*mes compagnons du mouvement symboliste.*" [74] This is not to say that Claudel was a mere imitator of Mallarmé or that his art can be explained as a flat application of symbolist poetics. He accepted Mallarmé's method but not his skepticism, and to the notion that the universe is a vast mystery to which the poet gives symbolic utterance, he added his conviction that these mysterious symbols can be deciphered and fully known. It is his faith in the poet's power to grasp and render wholly intelligible the hidden meaning of the universe that distinguishes Claudel from Mallarmé and the symbolists.[75]

Claudel's drama, like all of his writings, is far too personal and individualistic in both theme and expression to be explained as part of the symbolist or any other literary movement. Furthermore, it is impossible to isolate any single literary force or dominant influence in his dramatic art. The Greeks, the medieval liturgical drama, Shakespeare, Calderón, the classical French theater, and Wagner move side by side in Claudel's theater with the more proximate symbolist influences of Villiers, Mallarmé, and their followers. In several important respects, Claudel is a symbolist playwright, and his dramatic career is part of the same effort to reunite poetry and the theater that we have seen in Mallarmé and his followers. Yet, he is to be distinguished from them, not only in his conscious didacticism as a Catholic poet, but also because of the success and impact of his drama in the twentieth-century theater. As Jean-Richard Bloch declared, "Claudel est peut-être le seul parmi les grands lyriques du demi-siècle dernier qui laisse une œuvre théâtrale vivante." [76] The affinities of Claudel and the symbolists find expression as vividly in his theater as in his poetics and poetry, and they help to provide yet further illustration of the assimilation of symbolist values in the theater of the late nineteenth and early twentieth centuries.

Claudel made his debut as a playwright with *Tête d'Or*, written in 1889 and published anonymously in an edition of 300 copies in 1890.[77] It is an unusual play, mystifying in its structure and symbolic implications; yet as the recent production in Paris of Jean-Louis Barrault revealed, its powerful rhythm of action and emotion is absorbing and moving in the theater. It is important for us to view *Tête d'Or* within the development of Claudel as a religious playwright; alone among his plays, it is a drama suspended between the secular and the sacred.[78] In a letter of 1891 to Albert Mockel, the playwright dwelled at length on the controlling conceptions of his piece. It was written, he declared, out of an "*immense besoin de bonheur*" and out of his realization of the impossibility of satisfying this need "*parmi les choses visibles.*"[79] In this sense, the drama is a demonstration of the futility of grandeur without God, and it points unmistakably toward the religious preachment of all of Claudel's subsequent work. The exaltation of the hero and the spectacle of radical individualism in *Tête d'Or* suggest anarchistic implications, but the conclusion of the drama asserts a positive recognition of the limits of man before the spiritual immensity of the universe.

Tête d'Or seems to have attracted attention only within the *cénacle* of the young symbolists. The letters of Maeterlinck and Mockel to the young author bear witness to the play's profound and at the same time disconcerting effect. Octave Mirbeau accurately described it as "*heurté, violent, incohérent et génial.*"[80] The fluid and turbulent movement of the narrative, in sharp contrast to traditional patterns of dramatic action, the broad themes, and pervasive cosmic symbolism made the drama seem all but incomprehensible even to its warmest admirers. Far more violently than any of the symbolists, Claudel broke with the restrictions of the stage in his day. Mallarmé, recognizing the young playwright's originality and independence, saw *Tête d'Or* as a drama of the mind rather than as a play for stage performance. In his letter of January 5, 1891, Mallarmé declared prophetically:

> Le Théâtre, certes, est en vous.
>
> Un développement du geste des héros accompagne mystérieux ce rythme, d'instinct si vrai, par vous trouvé, moral autant que d'oreille, lequel commande l'imaginaire spectacle.
>
> L'autorité de vos personnages me hante, particulièrement; à travers le drame opiniâtre et sérieux et simple, où tout porte absolument votre marque, mon cher Claudel. Je vous sais, mais devinais.[81]

Nowhere is the solidity and penetration of Mallarmé's dramatic criticism more evident. These words of praise are not merely perfunctory; they express a profound realization of the unusual gifts of the young poet and of the force and grandeur of his art.

This is not to suggest that *Tête d'Or* or any of Claudel's plays represents a literal expression of Mallarmé's dramatic ideal. The broad, panoramic quality of the action is at sharp variance with Mallarmé's more restricted and more intimate conception of drama. Nevertheless, symbolist values are present. The opening scene of *Tête d'Or* presents virtually nothing by way of anecdote or narrative. The characters exist in themselves, apart from any background of events that enters into the substance of the play. In his letter to Mockel, Claudel made it clear that his characters are in fact embodiments of ideas:

> Cébès est l'homme ancien par rapport à l'homme nouveau, et aussi la faiblesse pitoyable. . . . La Princesse, outre son rang scénique, représente toutes les idées de douceur et de suavité: l'âme, la femme, la Sagesse, la Piété. L'Empereur est l'homme soumis à l'habitude du passé.[82]

In addition to this broad symbolization, close to allegory, the rhythmic and incantatory utterances that express the feelings or the " *états d'âme* " of the characters mark yet another element of symbolist dramaturgy in the play. The characters do not serve primarily to convey events or propel the action. The drama is essentially an inner drama: the interplay of both natural and supernatural forces. The plot is simple and even sparse; time and place are indefinite, and moods or attitudes dominate over action. *Tête d'Or* is not altogether a static drama; yet it exhibits marked affinities with the contemporary plays of Maeterlinck. There is a close kinship between the Princess of *Tête d'Or* and the Princess Maleine.[83] Both Claudel and Maeterlinck turn sharply away from linear and literal representation, to explore the interplay of the visible and invisible realms of being. Claudel's drama, as he conceived it, constitutes " *l'épuisement de la* conversation intérieure." [84]

Along with the mystery, suggestiveness, and spirituality characteristic of symbolist drama, we can see in Claudel's theater the same preoccupation with Wagner and the interrelations of the arts that we examined in Mallarmé. Claudel's response was that of his master. Like virtually all the young writers of the day, Claudel recognized and shared the "*reten-tissement*" of Wagner "*sur les nerfs de notre génération.*"[85] Romain Rolland remarked of him in 1889, "Il se dit Wagnérien," but he adds at once that Claudel claims to share none of Wagner's ideas.[86] In his subsequent career, Claudel came to view Wagner with increasing hostility. His criticism of Wagner's reduction of poetry in the theater, for the sake of music, and his counter-claim that poetry contains its own music are views derived directly from Mallarmé.[87] Like his master, Claudel saw poetry at the center of dramatic representation, reinforced by the alliance of the associated arts of the theater.[88] This is particularly evident in the "*théâtre total*" of *Christophe Colomb*, written in direct opposition to the "*théâtre psychologique et bourgeois*" dominating the contemporary stage.[89] For Claudel as for all of the symbolist playwrights, Wagner helped to liberate the drama from the confinement of realistic representation. The theater of dramatic illusion gives way to broad symbolic evocations of ideological and spiritual values. In Claudel's theater, these symbolic utterances are derived not so much from ancient myth and legend as from the Bible and from church liturgy.[90] The notion of the theater as a temple and of the drama as ritual might well have been reinforced, if not initially suggested, by the assimilation of Wagner's music-drama to the ritual of the Mass which Claudel noted in the essays of the *Revue Wagnérienne*.[91] It is likely that Claudel's liturgical concept of drama took form independent of any direct impact of Mallarmé's aesthetic; nevertheless, the community of thought suggested by Mallarmé's "*Catholicisme*" and his notion of "*Pièce, office*" is further testimony of the pervasive affinity of their vision of dramatic art.

It is no accident that playwrights in the symbolist tradition, notably Claudel and W. B. Yeats, should have been deeply impressed by the Japanese Nō drama and found it easy to assimilate its techniques and values: "*la révérence, le respect, l'acceptation spontanée d'une supériorité inaccessible à l'intelligence, la compression de notre existence personnelle en présence du mystère qui nous entoure, la sensation d'une présence autour de nous qui exige la cérémonie et la précaution.*" [92] These are precisely the same values invoked in Mallarmé's ideal theater. In *Le Soulier de Satin* and *Christophe Colomb* as well as in more literal adaptations, Claudel drew directly on the structure and technique of the Nō drama. A poetic drama evoking the images and feelings of inner life, the Nō brought together all of the arts of the theater in an intimate ceremony. The ready assimilation of the Japanese dramatic form is further evidence of the desire of the symbolist playwrights to widen the boundaries of the drama through an imaginative exploitation of its resources. In his bold experimentation with new dramatic forms, Claudel helped lend support to Mallarmé's demand for a reorientation of the theater.

It is difficult to determine the precise extent of Mallarmé's influence on Claudel's dramatic theory or practice. Abundant stylistic similarities have been described in the early plays, notably in *La Ville*,[93] and there can be no doubt of "a remarkable kinship of outlook." [94] Both writers insisted on the primacy of a theater of magic and of visionary experience, evocative rather than descriptive, dramatizing the interplay of natural and supernatural planes of being, and bringing together all the arts of the theater within a complex poetic structure. While Mallarmé saw dramatic performance as a religious ceremony, Claudel made this ceremony specifically Catholic, and for Claudel, this difference overshadowed any purely artistic similarities. In a historical perspective, we may see his dramatic theory and practice as a significant example of the assimilation and diffusion of the symbolist drama as it had been defined by Mallarmé. Claudel's turbulent, incantatory art may be quite different from the art which Mallarmé personally sought to create, but it nonetheless embodies dramatic values which Mallarmé set forth as the foundation of a new theater. The special importance of Claudel lies in the fact that he was the most gifted dramatist of all the playwrights who developed under Mallarmé's inspiration. Had the author of *Tête d'Or* and *Le Soulier de Satin* been a less gifted playwright, his work might have been even more representative and, at the same time, less original. In the vigor and scope of his achievement, Claudel is among the relatively small number of symbolist playwrights who made an enduring contribution to the modern theater. There are other modes of dramatic expression with a validity of their own; but in its defense and illustration of the place of poetry in the theater, Claudel's drama is a powerful source of the continuing vitality of the symbolist drama in our own time.

Of all the symbolist poets and playwrights perhaps the closest to Mallarmé in dramatic conception was Henri de Régnier, whom Mallarmé singled out in the Huret *Enquête* of 1891 as the most gifted young poet of the day, "*devant qui je m'incline avec admiration*" (871). No poet gave more lyrical expression to the values of the symbolists, the "*goût du mystérieux, du fluide, de l'incertain, la magie musicale du vocable qui donne une valeur active à la suggestion*"; [95] it was with complete accuracy that Emile Verhaeren could describe Régnier in 1890 as "*le plus net poète symboliste qui soit en France.*" [96]

Régnier's *La Gardienne*, written in 1891 and performed at the Théâtre de l'Œuvre in 1894, is clearly a symbolist drama. Like Maeterlinck's early plays, it is essentially the evocation of a mood rather than a depiction of a series of events, but the language is far more lyrical than the idiom of the Belgian playwright, and the removal from the actual and contemporary is even more complete. The drama consists of the return of "Le Maître" from the battlefield and from the life of turbulent strife to the forest and castle of his youth wherein, he declares, "*mon âme est rentrée en le lieu de ses rêves.*" He turns away from the vainglory of military adventure to confront himself and his destiny, a lonely old man haunted by the pathos of a lost past, a time when he loved and was loved in return. In the shadows of the forest, as in a dream vision, the veiled figure of La Gardienne appears to admit the suppliant to the "*château de songe et de sagesse,*" wherein his soul may become one with its destiny. There is no dialog, no development of character relationships, only the juxtaposition of "*l'état d'âme*" of the aged hero to the image of his beloved.

Clearly, *La Gardienne* is closer to dramatic poetry than to poetic drama. A contemporary critic claimed that the pleasure of seeing Régnier's play is closer to that derived from a concert than from a theatrical performance.[97] If the static action and purely symbolic characterization militate against traditional notions of plot and character, the staging of Lugné-Poe's production served further to disconcert the spectators: actors concealed in the orchestra pit read the lines, while other actors silently mimed the bodily movements and gestures on the stage.[98] According to contemporary reports, the performance was almost broken up by a riot in the theater.[99] In retrospect, this is difficult to understand. The presentation of *La Gardienne* may have seemed strange and unusual, but the drama consists only of a brief single act and should not have taxed the patience of the audience unduly. Régnier's play illustrates some of the difficulties of applying Mallarmé's doctrines to the composition of a stage play, but the effort cannot be dismissed as futile. The rich evocation of atmosphere and suggestiveness of language were new resources in the drama of the day, and in time, they came to acquire a measure of acceptance as part of a new conception of dramatic art. It is not proper to view a symbolist lyric drama in the same way we view a full-length prose drama of realistic events. Régnier's play is an interesting example of symbolist poetic drama, in striking contrast to the anecdotal reportage of prose realism or the strident melodrama derived from Wagner and the operatic tradition. Régnier has none of the broad significance of Maeterlinck or Claudel in the modern theater; yet his plays, like many experiments of the 1890's, served to call attention to the areas of expression that had been repudiated by the great majority of nineteenth-century playwrights, but which subsequently came to be incorporated into the modern drama.

Late in life, looking back on the symbolist movement, Henri de Régnier declared, " *nous étions tous mallarmistes.*"[100] In view of Mallarmé's lifelong passion for the theater, it is surely no accident that in the 1890's virtually all of his disciples attempted to write for the stage. Mallarmé gave warm support to their efforts and to the programs of the Théâtre d'Art and

Théâtre de l'Œuvre,[101] under whose auspices many of the young symbolists gained production for their plays. In passing, we may note Mallarmé's genuine encouragement of the dramatic efforts of Rodenbach,[102] Francis Jammes,[103] and Emile Verhaeren,[104] along with many others. The failure of most of the symbolists to win popular acclaim in the theater was no failure at all in the eyes of Mallarmé, for whom drama was reserved *" au seul théâtre de nous mêmes,"* the theater of mystery and of silence, incapable of reduction to descriptive statement.

The break between Lugné-Poe and the symbolists in 1897 marked the end of a deliberate attempt to extend the premises and techniques of symbolist poetry to the theater.[105] If the Théâtre de l'Œuvre was largely a coterie theater, demanding an act of imaginative sympathy as well as a concern with subtleties and nuances that could only be the property of an initiated elite, it was nevertheless a means by which the new poetic dramatists could find expression. And if the state of poetic drama in recent times may be described as playwrights in search of a theater, the converse was true, at least for a time, during the early years of the Théâtre de l'Œuvre. Lugné-Poe may have passed over some symbolist drama worthy of performance in order to champion the cause of Ibsen, whose plays he presented in symbolist style, but he also made every effort to encourage the symbolists to write for the stage. A letter of Stuart Merrill's to Gros, the manager of the Théâtre de l'Œuvre, illustrates the plight of the new dramatic impulse: " Dites à Lugné que je trouverai prochainement le titre de mon drame; après quoi je n'aurai plus qu'à trouver le drame ... et à l'écrire." [106] The failure of the symbolist playwrights in France to produce a sustained body of drama undoubtedly led to the break of 1897; and with the death of Mallarmé in 1898, the group lost its center of cohesion. The subsequent dramatic efforts of the symbolists were sporadic, disconnected, and primarily individual manifestations.

We cannot say that the inadequacies of the symbolist drama in France in the 1890's resulted from a lack of playwrights. There were many playwrights who shared Mallarmé's vision of a new poetic and symbolist drama and who tried to give this vision expression in their work: Vielé-Griffin, Van Lerberghe, Maeterlinck, Claudel, Régnier, Rodenbach, Jammes, Gide, Verhaeren, Saint-Pol-Roux, and many others of very considerable talent participated in this enterprise. If orthodox critics like Sarcey roundly condemned the productions of the Théâtre de l'Œuvre as undramatic and foreign to the stage, a more perceptive observer, Bernard Shaw, could write: " In the Théâtre de l'Œuvre there is not merely the ordinary theatrical intention, but a vigilant artistic conscience in the diction, the stage action, and the stage picture, producing a true poetic atmosphere, and triumphing easily over shabby appointments and ridiculous incidents." [107] In the 1890's the symbolist drama was a source of vitality and freshness amid the dreary repetitions of the theater of fashionable entertainment. The values inherent in the dramatic conceptions of Mallarmé and his followers were intrinsically important, fraught with immense consequences for the art of the stage. The failure of the symbolist drama to dominate the theater of the day should not blind us to its promise and its accomplishments. Perhaps none of the symbolist playwrights was a dramatist of genius, but many were writers of considerable talent whose work can still be viewed with interest and, at times, with animation and wonder. The existence of a symbolist drama, its achievement as well as its failure, is due in large part to the effort of the poet of *Hérodiade*. After the work of Mallarmé's followers, the symbolist example might be passionately embraced or just as violently condemned; it could not be ignored.

VI

MALLARMÉ'S DRAMATIC HERITAGE

ANY EVALUATION OF MALLARMÉ'S IMPACT
on the development of a symbolist drama is bound to be mixed.
At first glance, the disproportion between the poet's aspirations
and his accomplishments is almost staggering. The most ardent
admirer of Mallarmé's poetry could not claim for him a position
of eminence among the great dramatic writers of European
literature. If we feel that the author of *Hérodiade* and the *Faune*
"Intermède" had genuine dramatic gifts that were not developed, we still must view his achievement in the theater with
reservations and regrets: his effort is far more important than
its immediate consequences. Like Banville, whose aims and
values he shared, Mallarmé could have justly declared: "*j'ai dû
me borner à indiquer une route, qu'un autre poëte trouvera.*"[1]
Conscious of his inadequacies, in his elaborate vision of an ideal
drama Mallarmé expressed the counterpart of what he was unable to create. Yet, the vision was no idle fantasy, but an appeal
to other like-minded poets to help complete the task which he
had begun.

For Mallarmé, the involvement in the theater cannot be
separated from the pursuit of poetry. As we have seen in our
discussion of the abortive efforts of 1865, the playwright's loss
was the poet's gain. We may deplore Mallarmé's too easy
abandonment of the stage, but his passionate interest in the
drama remains at the heart of an added complexity and richness

in his poetry. Without this passionate involvement we would not have *Hérodiade* or "*L'Après-midi d'un Faune*," compositions that rank among the highest achievements of dramatic poetry of the last hundred years.

Dramatic poetry is not poetic drama, but the line of demarcation is fluid and imprecise. Poetic drama in our time is often equated with verse drama; yet a wider view would suggest that any drama in which language is organically part of the total configuration or structure of the work is perforce poetic drama, whether or not the lines rhyme. On the other hand, drama is a permanent element of poetry, as it is of fiction and other literary forms. We must not assume that the dominant genres of a particular epoch, even of our own, have any universal or permanent validity. Mallarmé saw poetry at the center of all imaginative expression and the separation of poetry from the theater as a misfortune that all poets should strive to remedy. Therefore, the dramatic poem represents an effort to keep alive the ancient alliance between poetry and drama until the conditions of the theater will again make possible their dynamic interplay. Mallarmé saw in the restrictions of the contemporary stage the principal barrier to the reunion of poet and playwright; his dramatic theory is an effort to sweep away these restrictions through a redefinition of the province of the stage and the nature of dramatic performance.

Mallarmé may be considered the inventor of a new dramatic theory that led to one of the few significant attempts in our time to transform the theater. We cannot claim that Mallarmé is exclusively responsible for the symbolist drama; yet in his personal role as well as in his programmatic declarations, he stands forth as the great synthesizer of a literary generation. His vision of what the theater could become is an expression of the originality of his poetic genius. No description of Mallarmé as the leading poet of the symbolist movement can take adequate account of this uniqueness. As Jean Cocteau has observed apropos of Mallarmé, "*les grands poètes résistent par quelqu'endroit solide aux étiquettes qu'on leur impose.*"[2] The originality of Mallarmé's mind and art transcends the restrictions and limits of a particular time or movement, even while it represents perhaps the highest achievement of its age.

Mallarmé did not consider himself the founder of symbolist drama, let alone the leader of a movement; but his intrinsic and his historical significance join hands as twin aspects of a larger underlying reality. The man and the poet move together. In Mallarmé the values of a symbolist drama were set forth as part of a total attitude toward life and art and these values were inculcated in his followers, particularly the young writers of his time. While the author of *Hérodiade* did not himself transform the theater, his disciples and adherents extended his dramatic vision and made it a living part of the resources of the modern stage. The theater of magic and wonder in the drama of our time is, to a considerable degree, the creation of Mallarmé.

The legacy of the poet can not be limited to his impact on his French and Belgian followers. Mallarmé's program for a reorientation of the theater bears witness to his consciousness of a profound crisis in the drama, which he sought to overcome. The fact that the rigorous opposition between poetry and reportage still prevails in the theater testifies to the failure of Mallarmé's program to effect a reformulation of the drama within the half century after his death. The poet-playwrights who subscribed to the premises of a symbolist drama and who sought to incorporate its values into their personal artistic vision encountered the same opposition between the literary and the theatrical, between coterie drama and mass drama, that we have seen in Mallarmé's experience. The "*lyrische Dramen*" of Hugo von Hofmannsthal,[3] the poetic drama—especially the "Plays for Dancers"—of W. B. Yeats,[4] and the work of such varied playwrights as Strindberg, García Lorca, Ghelderode, and Beckett, are proof of the persistence of the effort to overcome the mediocrity of purely representational drama through musicality and suggestiveness in both language and dramatic design, through a fluid interweaving of the planes of the everyday and the occult, through a reduction of the role of narrative, and through an interiorization of dramatic action. The theory and technique of symbolist drama

131

have been essential parts of the attempts of gifted experimental playwrights to widen the boundaries of the stage.

If at times Mallarmé insisted on a rigorous distinction between literary drama and the drama of theatrical performance, it should not be inferred from this that he sought to abolish the physical theater. Mallarmé loved the theater and was fascinated by it; but a drama on the stage, even in the moment of performance, was at once transformed by the poet into a suggestion or an evocation of an ideal theater. For Mallarmé the artistic quality of any particular drama depended, above all, on its possibilities of inner transformation. It is perfectly true that the poet and his disciples hoped to create a drama that would give the same pleasure when read or acted,⁵ but all of these playwrights aspired to gain production for their work. Mallarmé did not urge the poet to shun the theater, but rather to involve himself in it and help to bring about its reformation.⁶ This can come about, he insists, not through the emulation of fashionable popular successes, but through a radical break with the theory and technical processes of realistic representation.

The problem of Mallarmé's effort in the theater is essentially the problem of a symbolist drama: in what way can the poetics issuing from Poe and Baudelaire be brought into harmony with the art of the drama? The values of suggestiveness, musicality, mystery, reverie, and dream all point to an indifference to character and to human relationships, which have been a central part of the drama from ancient times to the present. Mallarmé's reflections on *Hamlet* would suggest that if he depreciated character relationships, he still considered character an important element of drama, not, however, for its expression of a purely personal history, but rather for its revelation of the antagonism of dream and fatality which is a universal condition of our existence. As Paul Valéry pointed out, the liturgical and ceremonial conception of theater methodically excludes any direct imitation of life on the stage, as obscuring the deeper meaning of the work.⁷ Nevertheless, we must see this opposition to the literal and anecdotal as an emphasis rather than an absolute injunction. The playwrights who most successfully drew upon the symbolist aesthetic did not repudiate the claims of material existence, but combined the actual and the ideal in an evocative pattern of dramatic action. Movement in the symbolist drama may be subdued, but even in the most "static" of symbolist plays, it is not altogether eliminated. In an absolute sense, symbolist drama may have been unrealizable: "*un théâtre symboliste qui n'était symboliste qu'à la condition de n'être pas théâtre.*" [8] There are plainly un-resolved—and perhaps unresolvable—tensions in the practical consequences of a symbolist dramaturgy, but we should not blame the symbolists for failing to emulate the followers of Scribe and Sardou. In any evaluation of the symbolists in the theater, the degree of individual talent is a matter of crucial importance. Many of the symbolist playwrights were not with-out genuine talent for the theater; yet the gap between their ambitions and their realization is immense. The achievements were all too few alongside the numerous failures; nevertheless, the attempt itself is of enduring significance in the development of the modern drama.

It has been claimed that "lyric drama emerges perhaps the one great artistic contribution, not of symbolism but of sym-bolists, to French literature." [9] This statement says both too much and too little. The great achievement of the symbolists lies in lyric poetry, and it is surely not too much to say that the character of twentieth-century poetry would be entirely different were it not for the efforts of three generations of unusually gifted symbolist poets. In our concern with sym-bolist drama we should not exaggerate its importance. On the other hand, we should not limit the contribution of symbolist drama to France and French literature. Throughout the western world, in drama as in lyric poetry, the symbolists encouraged inventiveness and experimentation; the demand for a new ideal theater was not a retreat from "reality" but an assertion of the variety and freedom of the playwright's art. It would be wrong to see Mallarmé and his followers as prisoners of their aesthetic theories. The symbolist theory of drama served to emphasize certain values and techniques, but from the very beginning, symbolist drama was individualistic and iconoclastic, free from the crude dependence on visual effectiveness and immediate popular success. Mallarmé's observations on the theater are animated by the poet's awareness of the possibilities of a new dramatic art; his meditations are as stimulating and pertinent today as when they were written, and we may find them at the origin of much of the reflection on the drama in our time.[10]

Mallarmé's vision of the theater remains an inaccessible ideal, but this does not diminish the grandeur of the poet's attempt or the deep significance of his critique of the modern stage. For Mallarmé, the theater is coexistent with the whole of experience, a momentary revelation of the mystery of existence, a clue to its ultimate meaning. It is for this reason that Mallarmé could declare: " Je pense que le monde sera sauvé par une meilleure littérature." [11] It is not through the propagation of creeds or slogans that the art of drama will contribute to man's salvation, but rather through the total enlargement and exaltation of being that is possible alone in " *notre seule magnificence, la scène.*"

NOTES

ABBREVIATIONS

BOOKS:

Corr. Stéphane Mallarmé, *Correspondance* 1862-1871, recueillie, classée et annotée par Henri Mondor, avec la collaboration de Jean-Pierre Richard (Paris, 1959).

O. c. Stéphane Mallarmé, *Œuvres complètes*, texte établi et annoté par Henri Mondor et G. Jean-Aubry, Bibliothèque de la Pléiade (Paris, 1956).

PERIODICALS:

CAIEF *Cahiers de l'Association Internationale des Etudes Françaises*
MF *Mercure de France*
NRF *Nouvelle Revue Française*
RHLF *Revue d'Histoire Littéraire de la France*
RI *Revue Indépendante*
RLC *Revue de Littérature Comparée*
RW *Revue Wagnérienne*

CHAPTER I

1. Albert Thibaudet, *La Poésie de Stéphane Mallarmé* (Paris, 1926), p. 93.
2. Page references in parentheses are to Mallarmé, *Œuvres complètes* (Paris, 1956). Texte établi et annoté par Henri Mondor et G. Jean-Aubry.
3. It is curious that this subject has received little detailed examination. The best general discussion remains that of Thibaudet, *op. cit.*, pp. 364-83. I have not seen the unpublished dissertation of Marilyn M. Barthelme, *Formation et mise en œuvre de la pensée de Mallarmé sur le théâtre* (Paris, 1959). A summary appears in *Annales de l'Université de Paris*, XXX (1960), 162-63.
4. Henri Mondor, *Mallarmé Lycéen* (Paris, 1954), p. 330.
5. It is reprinted in *ibid.*, pp. 152-55.
6. See Lloyd James Austin, "Les Années d'Apprentissage de Stéphane Mallarmé," *RHLF*, 56 (1956), 71.
7. Mondor, *Mallarmé Lycéen*, p. 152, ll. 9-10.

8. See *Corr.*, p. 25, n. 1. The discovery of these chronicles was made by Marilyn M. Barthelme in 1958.

9. *Ibid.*, p. 105.

10. See Robert Vivier, "La Victoire de Mallarmé," *Empreintes*, No. 5 (1948), 92; also, Pierre Beausire, *Mallarmé: Poésie et Poétique* (Lausanne, 1949), p. 59.

11. See Mondor, *Histoire d'un Faune* (Paris, 1948), p. 76.

12. *Corr.*, p. 109, n. 3.

13. Henri Mondor in *O. c.*, p. 1588.

14. Mallarmé's early admiration for Banville's theater is pointed out by René Ghil, *Les Dates et les Œuvres* (Paris, 1923), pp. 223-25. For an account of Mallarmé's veneration of Banville near the end of his career, see André Fontainas, *De Stéphane Mallarmé à Paul Valéry* (Paris, 1928), entry for le 1er avril 1896.

15. Henri Mondor asserts that Mallarmé owned the 1864 edition of this work, *Histoire d'un Faune*, p. 79.

16. Banville, *Comédies* (Paris, 1923), I, 168.

17. *Ibid.*, p. 211.

18. See Kurt Wais, *Mallarmé* (München, 1952), pp. 157-59.

19. Villiers de l'Isle-Adam, *Isis* (Paris, 1862), p. 80.

20. For proof that Mallarmé knew *Isis*, see Mondor, *Eugène Lefébure* (Paris, 1951), p. 196. Kurt Wais' contention (*op. cit.*, p. 157) that Mallarmé read the book in 1862 is probably correct.

21. See the letter of Aubanel of August 6, 1865, in *Corr.*, p. 171, n. 2.

22. *Corr.*, p. 221.

23. Thibaudet, *op. cit.*, p. 390.

24. E. Noulet, *L'Œuvre poétique de Stéphane Mallarmé* (Paris, 1940), p. 106.

25. *Corr.*, pp. 154; 160.

26. *O. c.*, p. 1544.

27. Mondor, *Vie de Mallarmé* (Paris, 1941), p. 161. Publication of the correspondence between Banville and Mallarmé would be of inestimable value.

28. *Corr.*, p. 174.

29. *Corr.*, p. 137.

30. Cf. Guy Michaud, *Mallarmé, l'homme et l'œuvre* (Paris, 1953), p. 36.

31. See Gardner Davies, "Introduction" to Mallarmé, *Les Noces d'Hérodiade* (Paris, 1959), p. 14.

32. Davies, *op. cit.*, p. 24.

33. For a more detailed discussion of the "Ouverture," see the fine analysis of A. R. Chisholm in *Towards Hérodiade* (Melbourne, 1934), pp. 151-56.

34. Mallarmé's notation concerning the nurse on the manuscript of the "Ouverture": "Elle déplore l'absence d'une princesse," points to

the presence of additional narrative and psychological elements, but the reader's familiarity with the details of the plot is assumed, here and throughout. Cf. Davies, *op. cit.*, p. 26.

35. Robert Kemp, *La Vie du Théâtre* (Paris, 1956), p. 18.
36. The manuscript is reproduced in *O. c.*, p. 1444.
37. Robert de Montesquiou, *Diptyque de Flandre, Triptyque de France* (Paris, 1921), p. 231. Cf. Davies, *op. cit.*, p. 32.
38. For contemporary parallels of the mirror symbol, see Chisholm, *op. cit.*, pp. 144-46; also, cf. Guy Michaud, " Le thème du miroir dans le symbolisme français," *CAIEF*, 11 (1959), 199-216; and Austin Gill, " Le symbole du miroir dans l'œuvre de Mallarmé," *ibid.*, pp. 159-81.
39. Noulet, *op. cit.*, p. 103; Wais, *op. cit.*, p. 174.
40. Montesquiou, *op. cit.*, p. 235. Kurt Wais dates this plan as of 1879 (*op. cit.*, p. 164), but Montesquiou provides no precise indication. The description is supported by the texts published in *Les Noces d'Hérodiade*. See Davies, *op. cit.*, p. 16.
41. *Ibid.*, p. 40.
42. For a detailed and illuminating discussion, see L. J. Austin, " Le ' Cantique de Saint Jean ' de Stéphane Mallarmé," *AUMLA*, No. 10 (May, 1959), 46-59.
43. *Ibid.*, p. 53.
44. Cited in *Corr.*, p. 176, n.
45. *Ibid.*, p. 153.
46. See Mondor, *Eugène Lefébure*, p. 286.
47. Kenneth Cornell, *The Symbolist Movement* (New Haven, 1951), p. 13.
48. Cf. *O. c.*, p. 1444.
49. Mondor, *Vie de Mallarmé*, p. 801.
50. Davies, *op. cit.*, p. 21.
51. *Ibid.*, p. 17; also see p. 28.
52. Mallarmé, *Les Noces d'Hérodiade*, p. 95.
53. *Ibid.*, p. 118.
54. *Ibid.*, p. 51.
55. *Corr.*, p. 154.
56. Mallarmé, *Les Noces d'Hérodiade*, p. 94.
57. *Ibid.*, p. 93.
58. For the popularity of *Hérodiade* and its impact on Mallarmé's symbolist disciples, see Wais, *op. cit.*, p. 174.
59. Cf. Kemp, *op. cit.*, pp. 20-21.
60. See Dorothy Knowles, *La Réaction Idéaliste au Théâtre depuis 1890* (Paris, 1934), p. 428.
61. See *Empreintes*, No. 10-11 (nov.-déc., 1948), p. 60.
62. See the review by Robert Kemp, *op. cit.*, pp. 18-25.
63. See *Corr.*, p. 242.

64. Remy de Gourmont, *Le Problème du Style* (Paris, 1924), p. 201.
65. See *Corr.*, p. 166.
66. Excerpts from Banville's letter to Mallarmé may be found in Mondor, *Histoire d'un Faune*, p. 100.
67. *Corr.*, p. 169.
68. See Mondor, *Vie de Mallarmé*, p. 169; also, *Corr.*, p. 171, n. 2.
69. *Corr.*, p. 174.
70. Des Essarts' letter is cited in *O. c.*, p. 1454.
71. *Corr.*, p. 208.
72. It is to be hoped that the text of *Le Reveil du Faune*, Editions Rombaldi (Paris, 1944), along with other sections of Mallarmé's "Intermède," will soon be made readily available.
73. Henri Mondor in *Histoire d'un Faune*, pp. 99 and 104, suggests the contrary, but the recently published fragments do not support his conjecture.
74. Henri Mondor suggests the date of 1865 in *O. c.*, p. 1450. Legitimate doubts are expressed by Antoine Fongaro, "L'Après-midi d'un Faune et le Second Faust," *Revue des Sciences Humaines*, Fasc. 83 (juillet-septembre 1956), p. 327, n. 3. The absence of the phrase, "duo de vierges quand je vins" in the "Dialogue des Nymphes" published in *Les Lettres* (1948), p. 21, seems to me crucial. It implies that while in the poem of 1876 the faun ravished the virgins, in the "Intermède" of 1865 he did not. His agitation and the fears expressed by the nymphs in their dialog seem to lend support to this view.
75. *Corr.*, p. 169.
76. It is difficult to see how Kurt Wais can write of "allen 187 Versen in ihrer Gesamtheit," in his essay, "Die Szenenfolge von Mallarmés Syrinx-Drama und die Hirtentragödie Aubanels," *Französische Marksteine von Racine bis Saint-John Perse* (Berlin, 1958), p. 278.
77. The "Dialogue des Nymphes" (52 lines) is reprinted in *Les Lettres, Numéro Spécial: Stéphane Mallarmé*, III (1948), 21-23. A fragment of the final monolog of *Le Reveil du Faune* is reprinted under the title, "Inédit de Mallarmé" (18 lines) in *Empreintes*, No. 5 (nov.-déc. 1948), pp. 12-13.
78. For a comparison of the various published texts, see Kurt Wais, "Die Szenenfolge von Mallarmés Syrinx-Drama . . . ," pp. 287-95, n. 14-39.
79. See *Corr.*, p. 169, n. 1.
80. *Corr.*, p. 169.
81. See *Corr.*, p. 168.
82. Mallarmé did not always hold this view. For his insistence on separation and purity of genres, see his letter to Anatole France of May 15, 1876, in *Propos sur la Poésie* (Monaco, 1953), p. 119.
83. *Corr.*, p. 169. This interaction was often a source of difficulty of composition. See *Corr.*, p. 171.

84. For a detailed study, see Howard Lee Nostrand, *Le théâtre antique et à l'antique en France de 1840 à 1900* (Paris, 1934).
85. Robert Vivier, " Mallarmé le Parnassien," *Cahiers du Nord*, 21 (1948), 198.
86. See Wais, "Die Szenenfolge von Mallarmés Syrinx-Drama . . . ," pp. 284-85.
87. Cf. Gianfranco Contini, " Sulla trasformazione dell' ' Après-midi d'un Faune,' " *L'Immagine*, II, No. 9-10 (agosto-dicembre 1948), 509-11. Also see Wais, *op. cit.*, pp. 283-90.
88. Mondor, *Histoire d'un Faune*, p. 79.
89. Cited by Wais, *Mallarmé*, p. 226.
90. As in Mondor, *Histoire d'un Faune*, p. 84.
91. The problem is discussed in detail by Kurt Wais, " Die Szenenfolge von Mallarmés Syrinx-Drama . . . ," whose conclusions are cautious and reasonable.
92. This view is set forth by Joseph Winkel, *Mallarmé-Wagner-Wagnerismus* (Bückeburg, 1935), pp. 59-62.
93. Wais, *Mallarmé*, pp. 239 and 672, n. 4.
94. See Austin Gill, " Mallarmé et l'antiquité: L'Après-midi d'un faune," *CAIEF* (1958), pp. 170-71.
95. See Robert Gavelle, " Goethe et Mallarmé ou les secrets du Faune," *Cahiers du Sud* (1951), 150-54; and Antoine Fongaro, " L'Après-midi d'un Faune et le Second Faust," *Revue des Sciences Humaines*, Fasc. 83 (juillet-septembre 1956), 327-32.
96. Cf. *Corr.*, p. 159, n. 1.
97. *Ibid.*, p. 153.
98. Gavelle, *op. cit.*, p. 150. This is a reasonable view, although no evidence is presented for it.
99. See Fongaro, *op. cit.*, p. 332.
100. *Loc. cit.*
101. See Fernand Baldensperger, *Goethe en France* (Paris, 1904), pp. 143-47.
102. *Corr.*, p. 166.
103. " Inédit de Mallarmé," *Empreintes*, No. 5 (nov.-déc. 1948), pp. 12-13.
104. *Corr.*, p. 169.
105. Wais, *Mallarmé*, pp. 233-35. The text of the Rombaldi edition makes it clear that from the beginning Mallarmé thought of his Faun as a musician, chosen by art.
106. *Corr.*, p. 169.
107. Gardner Davies, *Vers une explication rationnelle du ' Coup de Dés '* (Paris, 1953), p. 46 and n. 1.
108. Wais, " Die Szenenfolge von Mallarmés Syrinx-Drama . . . ," p. 279.
109. See Noulet, *op. cit.*, p. 232; Charly Guyot, " La genèse de l'après-midi d'un faune," in *Stéphane Mallarmé: Essais et Temoignages*

(Neuchâtel, 1942), pp. 93-103.
110. Michaud, *Mallarmé*, p. 99.
111. For a recent example, see Jacques Scherer, *Le " Livre " de Mallarmé* (Paris, 1957), pp. 23-24.
112. The letter is published in *Empreintes*, No. 10-11 (septembre-octobre 1952), p. 81.
113. *O. c.*, p. 1463.
114. For the argument of Nijinsky's ballet and its relation to Mallarmé, see Thomas Munro, " The Afternoon of a Faun and the Interrelation of the Arts," *Journal of Aesthetics and Art Criticism*, X (1951), 101.
115. Noulet, *op. cit.*, p. 223.
116. Vivier, " Mallarmé le Parnassien," *loc. cit.*, p. 198.

CHAPTER II

1. *Corr.*, p. 165 and n. 2.
2. See Mondor, *Eugène Lefébure*, pp. 225-29.
3. *Corr.*, pp. 259-60.
4. Villiers called Mallarmé's attention to his preface to *Morgane* in a letter of January 1866. See G. Jean-Aubry, *Une Amitié Exemplaire: Villiers de l'Isle-Adam et Stéphane Mallarmé* (Paris, 1942), p. 27.
5. Villiers made vigorous but unsuccessful efforts to interest theater directors in producing *Morgane*. See P.-G. Castex and A. W. Raitt, " De ' Morgane ' au ' Prétendant ' " in Castex (ed.), *Autour du Symbolisme* (Paris, 1955), p. 26.
6. *Corr.*, p. 174.
7. *Corr.*, p. 313.
8. Cf. Mondor, *Vie de Mallarmé*, p. 300 and *Corr.*, p. 331, n. 2.
9. The order of the parts of *Igitur* is questioned, for example, by A. Orliac, *Mallarmé: tel qu'en lui-même* (Paris, 1948), p. 72.
10. Henri de Régnier, *Proses datées* (Paris, 1925), p. 33.
11. Paul Claudel, " La Catastrophe d'*Igitur*," *NRF* (1926), 533.
12. See Orliac, *op. cit.*, p. 90.
13. C. Chassé, " Le Thème de Hamlet chez Mallarmé," in *Autour du Symbolisme*, p. 163. Cf. Orliac, *op. cit.*, pp. 81-82; and Wallace Fowlie, *Mallarmé* (Chicago, 1953), pp. 105-18.
14. See Jean Royère, *Mallarmé* (1931), p. 174.
15. Orliac, *op. cit.*, p. 75.
16. Chassé, *op. cit.*, pp. 166-67.
17. Royère, *op. cit.*, p. 175.
18. Cf. Beausire, *op. cit.*, p. 69.
19. This is the view of Jean Royère, *op. cit.*, p. 177, and of Maurice Blanchot, " L'Experience d'*Igitur*," in *L'Espace Littéraire* (Paris, 1955), p. 117.

20. The "Cornet . . . d'unicorne," in its traditional suggestion of virginity as well as of mystery and magic, is a symbol of this purity. See Odell Shepard, *The Lore of the Unicorn* (Boston, 1930), pp. 73; 273-78.
21. Royère, *op. cit.*, p. 177.
22. Cf. Wais, *op. cit.*, p. 217.
23. Beausire, *op. cit.*, p. 71.
24. *Ibid.*, p. 79.
25. The relationship of *Igitur* and *Axël* is discussed in illuminating detail by Wais in *Mallarmé*, pp. 220-23.
26. Edouard Dujardin, *Mallarmé par un des siens* (Paris, 1936), p. 72. Cf. E. Bonniot, "Préface," in Mallarmé, *O. c.*, p. 431; and Royère, *op. cit.*, p. 176.
27. See Scherer, *op. cit.*, *feuillets* 4 (A) and 5 (A). Cf. S. Bernard, *Mallarmé et la Musique* (Paris, 1959), p. 137 and n. 178.
28. Royère, *op. cit.*, p. 172.
29. *Corr.*, p. 327, n. 1.
30. *Corr.*, p. 343.
31. *Corr.*, p. 344.
32. *Corr.*, p. 347.
33. *Corr.*, p. 352.
34. *Corr.*, p. 323. Later in 1870 Villiers brought Mallarmé a copy of *La Révolte. Corr.*, p. 332.
35. *Corr.*, p. 354.
36. Cf. *Corr.*, pp. 352-53, n.
37. Cf. *Dix-neuf lettres de Stéphane Mallarmé à Émile Zola* (Paris, 1929), pp. 19-20.
38. *O. c.*, pp. 723-24; 802; 819.
39. Eileen Souffrin, "Coup d'oeil sur la Bibliothèque Anglaise de Mallarmé," *RLC* (1958), 393. The testimony of Charles Coligny is of interest. Writing of Mallarmé in *L'Artiste* in 1863, he declared, "Shakespeare et Edgar Poe sont ses dieux." See *Corr.*, p. 84, n. 1.
40. *Corr.*, p. 25.
41. Cf. Charles Chassé, "Le thème de *Hamlet* chez Mallarmé," p. 162.
42. See René Taupin, "The Myth of Hamlet in France in Mallarmé's Generation," *Modern Language Quarterly*, 14 (1953), 432-47.
43. See *Corr.*, pp. 245-48, and Wais, *Mallarmé*, pp. 186-89.
44. Émile Montégut, "Types Modernes en littérature: Hamlet," *Revue des Deux Mondes*, 1 avril 1856, p. 670. Cited by Chassé, *op. cit.*, p. 160.
45. Montégut, *op. cit.*, p. 666.
46. Henri Blaze de Bury, "Hamlet et ses commentateurs depuis Goethe," *Revue des Deux Mondes*, 15 mars 1868, p. 446.
47. Henri de Régnier, *Proses datées*, p. 22.

48. Cf. Taupin, *op. cit.*, pp. 443-44.
49. See Jean Noël, "George Moore et Mallarmé," *RLC*, 32 (1958), 363-76.
50. George Moore, "Souvenir sur Mallarmé," *Parsifal*, No. 3 (1909), pp. 36-37.
51. Noël, *op. cit.*, p. 370.
52. George Moore, *Avowals* (London, 1924), p. 264. Cf. Mondor, *Vie de Mallarmé*, p. 396.
53. Moore, "Souvenir sur Mallarmé," pp. 36-37.
54. *Ibid.*, p. 37.
55. Moore, *Avowals*, p. 263.
56. Cf. Dujardin, *Mallarmé par un des siens*, p. 73.
57. Cf. *Corr.*, pp. 153-54 and 159, n. 1.
58. *Corr.*, p. 154.
59. Taupin, *op. cit.*, pp. 434-35.
60. Cited by Mondor, *Vie de Mallarmé*, p. 376.
61. *Ibid.*, p. 377, n. 3.
62. Noël, *op. cit.*, p. 370.
63. Mondor, *Vie de Mallarmé*, p. 376.
64. A contrary view is suggested by Henri Mondor, *ibid.*, p. 397.
65. I am very grateful to my friend and colleague, William T. Bandy, for the excerpts from Mallarmé's hitherto unpublished letters to Mrs. Sarah Whitman.
66. Cited by Mondor, *Vie de Mallarmé*, p. 396.

CHAPTER III

1. *Corr.*, p. 222.
2. *Ibid.*, p. 222, n. 3.
3. *Ibid.*, p. 226.
4. This is the view of A. G. Lehmann, *The Symbolist Aesthetic in France* (Oxford, 1950), pp. 232-33.
5. *Corr.*, p. 161.
6. See A. W. Raitt, "Autour d'une lettre de Mallarmé," in P.-G. Castex (ed.), *op. cit.*, pp. 149-50.
7. *Corr.*, p. 242.
8. See L. J. Austin, "Mallarmé et le rêve du 'Livre,'" *MF*, 317 (janvier, 1953), 81-108; Michaud, *Mallarmé*, pp. 57-61; Davies, *Vers une explication rationnelle du 'Coup de Dés,'* pp. 33-43.
9. Austin, *op. cit.*, p. 90.
10. *Corr.*, p. 153.
11. *Ibid.*, pp. 243-44. For a fuller discussion of Mallarmé's occultism, see Jacques Scherer, *L'Expression Littéraire dans l'Œuvre de Mallarmé* (Paris, 1947), pp. 155-62.

12. See Dmitrij Čiževskij, "Das Buch als Symbol des Kosmos," in *Aus zwei Welten* (The Hague, 1956), pp. 85-114.
13. Scherer suggests that Mallarmé began work on his "Livre" around 1873. See *Le "Livre" de Mallarmé*, p. 150.
14. Dujardin, *Mallarmé par un des siens*, p. 84.
15. Guy Delfel, *L'Esthétique de Stéphane Mallarmé* (Paris, 1951), p. 73.
16. See Raitt, "Autour d'une lettre de Mallarmé," p. 152.
17. A good general discussion is provided by E. Carcassonne, "Wagner et Mallarmé," *RLC*, 16 (1936), 347-66.
18. Arthur Symons, *The Symbolist Movement in Literature* (New York, 1958), p. 62.
19. Cf. Henri Mondor in *O. c.*, p. 1593.
20. The publication of *L'Art Romantique* is discussed by J. Crépet in Baudelaire, *L'Art Romantique* (Paris, 1925), p. 436.
21. *Corr.*, p. 245.
22. See Dujardin, *Mallarmé par un des siens*, pp. 196-97.
23. For an excellent discussion, see E. Drougard, "Richard Wagner et Villiers de l'Isle-Adam," *RLC*, 14 (1934), 297-330.
24. Cf. Villiers' letter to Baudelaire of 1861, wherein he declares, "Je me suis rencontré de vous au sujet de Wagner," in E. and J. Crépet, *Charles Baudelaire* (Paris, 1928), pp. 444-47. Also see E. de Rougemont, *Villiers de l'Isle-Adam* (Paris, 1910), p. 91, n. 1.
25. See René Dumesnil, "Villiers de l'Isle-Adam et Richard Wagner; lettres inédites à Jean Marras," *Revue de Paris*, 56 (juillet 1949), 20-35.
26. Drougard, *op. cit.*, p. 297.
27. *Corr.*, p. 326, n. 2.
28. Roger Lhombreaud, "Lettres inédites de Mallarmé," *MF*, 337 (novembre 1959), p. 477.
29. Mallarmé's letter of August 16, 1876 is reproduced in *Empreintes*, No. 10-11 (septembre-octobre 1952), p. 64.
30. Cf. *Corr.*, p. 318.
31. See Baudelaire, *L'Art Romantique*, p. 216.
32. For further arguments in support of Baudelaire's role as a mediator between Wagner and Mallarmé, see Delfel, *op. cit.*, pp. 125-26.
33. Cf. Kurt Jäckel, *Richard Wagner in der französischen Literatur* (Breslau, 1931), I, 19.
34. Fowlie, *op. cit.*, p. 84. For a strong statement of the contrary view, see Lehmann, *op. cit.*, pp. 194-206.
35. Dujardin, *Mallarmé par un des siens*, p. 212.
36. Cf. I. Wyzewska, *La Revue Wagnérienne* (Paris, 1934), p. 45.
37. Letter of July 5, 1885 to Edouard Dujardin, in *O. c.*, p. 1592.
38. Letter of June 27, 1884, reprinted in Mallarmé, *Propos sur la Poésie*, p. 134.
39. For discussion of Mallarmé's criticism of Wagner in the "Rêverie,"

see Carcassonne, *op. cit.*, p. 319; Lehmann, *op. cit.*, p. 230; L. J. Austin, "Le Principal Pilier, Mallarmé, Victor Hugo et Richard Wagner," *RHLF*, 51 (1951), 162-64. For a vigorous statement of differences between the two, see Julien Benda, "Mallarmé et Wagner," in *Domaine Français* (Genève, 1943), pp. 353-59.

40. Henri de Régnier, "Mallarmé au théâtre," *Journal des Débats*, 7 septembre 1908.

41. Charles Chassé, "Ce que Mallarmé pensait de la danse," *Les Lettres Nouvelles*, 4 (1956), 123.

42. Bernard, *Mallarmé et la Musique*, p. 65.

43. Cf. Lehmann, *op. cit.*, p. 205.

44. *O. c.*, p. 1592.

45. Bernard, *op. cit.*, p. 25.

46. Edouard Dujardin, "Les Œuvres théoriques de Richard Wagner," *RW*, 8 avril 1885, p. 67.

47. *RW*, 8 juillet 1885, p. 187.

48. Dujardin, *Mallarmé par un des siens*, p. 18.

49. Lehmann, *op. cit.*, p. 230.

50. Cf. Carcassonne, *op. cit.*, p. 355.

51. *O. c.*, p. 1496.

52. To this extent, I share the interpretation of Thibaudet, *op. cit.*, p. 307. The first two parts of the poem clearly evoke the old theater and the old poetry, now rejected.

53. See Lloyd James Austin, "Le Principal Pilier . . . ," pp. 154-80. This view was also suggested by Adolphe Boschot, "Le wagnérisme de Stéphane Mallarmé," *L'Echo de Paris*, 4 octobre 1923, p. 4. For the view that the phrase is an allusion to Wagner himself, see Gardner Davies, *Les "Tombeaux" de Mallarmé* (Paris, 1950), p. 139.

54. Mallarmé's letter is cited by Vittorio Pica in the *Gazzetta Letteraria* (Torino) for January 15, 1887. The relevant statements of the poet are reproduced by Olga Ragusa, *Mallarmé in Italy* (New York, 1957), pp. 67-68.

55. Wagner, "*Lettre sur la Musique*," in *Quatre Poèmes d'Opéras* (Paris, 1861), p. xxviii.

56. Cf. Erich Kloss, "Richard Wagner und die Tanzkunst," *Bühne und Welt*, 7 (1904-05), 993-99.

57. See Wagner, "*Lettre sur la Musique*," p. lxi.

58. *Richard Wagner an Mathilde Wesendonk* (Berlin, 1908), p. 224. Cf. Kloss, *op. cit.*, p. 995.

59. Dujardin, "Les Œuvres théoriques de Richard Wagner," p. 68.

60. Cf. Chassé, "Ce que Mallarmé pensait de la danse," p. 129; Wais, *Mallarmé*, p. 338.

61. Mallarmé, "Notes sur le théâtre," *RI*, III (avril 1887), 63.

62. See the letter of Houston Stewart Chamberlain to Cosima Wagner

of November 15, 1893, cited in Wais, *Mallarmé*, p. 320.

63. Henri de Régnier, "Souvenirs wagnériens," *Proses datées*, p. 45.

64. André Fontainas, *De Stéphane Mallarmé à Paul Valéry*, entry for le 18 janvier 1895.

65. Paul Valéry, "Situation de Baudelaire," *Œuvres* (Paris, 1957), I, 612.

66. Wais, *Mallarmé*, p. 271.

67. Bernard, *Mallarmé et la Musique*, p. 25.

68. For a representative early example, see Vittorio Pica, "Les Modernes Byzantins," *RI*, I (fevrier 1891), 180-83.

69. Camille Mauclair, *Princes de l'Esprit* (Paris, 1930), p. 105.

70. Georges Rodenbach, *L'Elite* (Paris, 1899), p. 52.

71. Typical examples are provided by Ghil, *op. cit.*, p. 238; Boschot, *op. cit.*, p. 4; Dujardin, *Mallarmé par un des siens*, p. 79; Jäckel, *op. cit.*, I, 114; Winkel, *op. cit.*, p. 21. Jäckel admits Mallarmé's reservations but claims that they are unimportant, *op. cit.*, I, 119.

72. A rapid examination of discussions of this view may be found in Delfel, *op. cit.*, pp. 25-30.

73. Cf. Lehmann, *op. cit.*, p. 230.

74. Mallarmé, "Notes sur le théâtre," *RI*, I (décembre 1886), 251.

75. Cf. Bernard, *op. cit.*, pp. 58 and 66.

76. Mallarmé, "Notes sur le théâtre," *RI*, II (janvier 1887), 56.

77. Cf. Delfel, *op. cit.*, p. 117.

78. *Dix-Neuf Lettres de Stéphane Mallarmé à Émile Zola*, p. 63.

79. Carcassonne, *op. cit.*, p. 357.

80. Mallarmé, "Notes sur le théâtre," *RI*, II (février 1887), 194.

81. *RI*, III (juin 1887), 370.

82. Cf. Bernard, *op. cit.*, p. 79.

83. Mallarmé, "Notes sur le théâtre," *RI*, III (juin 1887), 370.

84. This essay was incorporated into "Solennité" in *Crayonné au Théâtre*. Cf. *O. c.*, pp. 332-36.

85. Banville, *Le Forgeron* (Paris, 1887), p. 26.

86. Mallarmé, "Notes sur le théâtre," *RI*, III (juin 1887), 367. In subsequent editions, the text reads "supérieur" in place of "primitif." Cf. *O. c.*, p. 333.

87. Cf. Scherer, *Le "Livre" de Mallarmé*, p. 114.

88. Paul Margueritte, "Le printemps tourmenté," *Revue des Deux Mondes*, 51 (le 15 mai 1919), 244. Cf. Wais, *Mallarmé*, p. 339; *O. c.*, pp. 1511-12.

89. Mallarmé, "Notes sur le théâtre," *RI*, III (avril 1887), 61.

90. Margueritte, *op. cit.*, p. 246.

91. Cited in Mondor, *Vie de Mallarmé*, pp. 464-65.

92. See Ernst Robert Curtius, "The Book as Symbol," in *European Literature and the Latin Middle Ages* (New York, 1953), pp. 302-47; also, Čiževskij, *op. cit.*, pp. 85-114.

93. Čiževskij points to a similar reversal in the Russian symbolist poets, *ibid.*, p. 111.
94. For Mallarmé's elaboration of this view, see "Le Livre, Instrument Spirituel," *O. c.*, pp. 378-82.
95. Pica cited from Mallarmé's letter in an article on the poet in the *Gazzetta Letteraria* of November 27, 1886. The excerpt is reprinted as a fragment, "Sur le théâtre," in *O. c.*, pp. 875-76. Cf. Ragusa, *op. cit.*, p. 64.
96. Cf. Emilie Noulet, "Mallarmé et 'Le Livre,'" *Lettres Nouvelles*, V (1957), 339.
97. Cited in Mondor, *Vie de Mallarmé*, p. 505.
98. Henri de Régnier, *Figures et Caractères* (Paris, 1901), p. 142.
99. Pica, "Les Modernes Byzantins," *RI*, 18 (mars 1891), 316.
100. *Ibid.*, p. 357.
101. Cf. Ghil, *op. cit.*, pp. 233-44; Dujardin, *Mallarmé par un des siens*, p. 77.
102. *Ibid.*, p. 74.
103. Scherer, *Le "Livre" de Mallarmé*, pp. 31-34.
104. *Ibid.*, "Texte du Manuscrit," p. 129 (A).
105. *Ibid.*, p. 28.
106. Banville, *Critiques* (Paris, 1917), p. 258.
107. Scherer, *Le "Livre" de Mallarmé*, "Texte du Manuscrit," p. 83 (B).
108. *Ibid.*, p. 38.
109. *Ibid.*, p. 111.
110. Margueritte, *op. cit.*, p. 246.
111. Delfel, *op. cit.*, p. 175.
112. See Pica, "Les Modernes Byzantins," *RI*, 18 (mars 1891), 354-55; Ghil, *op. cit.*, p. 242; Mauclair, *Princes de l'Esprit*, p. 123; also see pp. 113-14; Jäckel, *op. cit.*, I, 121; Wais, *Mallarmé*, p. 338.
113. Lehmann, *op. cit.*, p. 232.
114. Dujardin, "Bayreuth," *RW*, 8 août 1885, p. 208.
115. Baudelaire, *L'Art Romantique*, p. 218.
116. Cf. Scherer, *op. cit.*, p. 79; "Texte du Manuscrit," p. 106 (A).
117. *O. c.*, p. 328.
118. See Dujardin, *Mallarmé par un des siens*, p. 81.
119. Paul Valéry, in a letter to Henri Mondor of March, 1942, cited in the "Préface" to Scherer, *Le "Livre" de Mallarmé*, p. xxiv; cf. Dujardin, *Mallarmé par un des siens*, p. 85.

CHAPTER IV

1. "Bibliographie" to *Divagations*, 1896, reprinted in *O. c.*, p. 1561.
2. Cited in "Notes sur le théâtre," *RI*, II (janvier 1887), 55.
3. *RI*, II (février 1887), 193.

4. *Ibid.*, p. 198.
5. *RI*, III (avril 1887), 60.
6. *RI*, III (mai 1887), 246-47.
7. *RI*, II (mars 1887), 390.
8. *RI*, IV (juillet 1887), 59.
9. *RI*, II (janvier 1887), 55.
10. *RI*, II (février 1887), 192.
11. *RI*, II (janvier 1887), 56.
12. *RI*, IV (juillet 1887), 58.
13. Cf. Austin Gill, "Le symbole du miroir dans l'œuvre de Mallarmé," *CAIEF*, 11 (1959), 171.
14. Bernard, *op. cit.*, p. 136; cf. Scherer, *Le " Livre " de Mallarmé*, p. 139 and " Texte du Manuscrit," p. 105.
15. Cf. Mauclair, *Princes de l'Esprit*, pp. 125-26.
16. Cf. Fowlie, *op. cit.*, pp. 241-42.
17. Henri de Régnier, " Mallarmé au théâtre," *Journal des Débats*, le 7 septembre 1908.
18. Cf. Bernard, *op. cit.*, p. 137.
19. See Jean Royère, "Commentaire," *Dix-Neuf Lettres de Stéphane Mallarmé à Émile Zola*, pp. 73-74. Also see Paul Bénichou, " Mallarmé et le public," *Cahiers du Sud*, 30 (1949), 286-89.
20. Cf. Carcassonne, *op. cit.*, pp. 354-55.
21. Scherer, Le " *Livre* " *de Mallarmé*, " Texte du Manuscrit," p. 89 (A).
22. *Ibid.*, p. 5 (A). For a more complex elaboration, see p. 70 (B). Also cf. *O. c.*, pp. 428-29; Robert Greer Cohn, *L'Œuvre de Mallarmé: Un Coup de Dés* (Paris, 1951), pp. 42-45; and Bernard, *op. cit.*, p. 137 and n. 178.
23. Cf. Wais, *Mallarmé*, p. 333.
24. *Corr.*, p. 166.
25. The classical statement of this position is Charles Lamb's essay of 1811, " On the Tragedies of Shakespeare, considered with reference to their fitness for Stage Representation."
26. See Henri Mondor, *Autres précisions sur Mallarmé et Inédits* (Paris, 1961), pp. 257-60.
27. Cf. Michaud, *Mallarmé*, p. 154.
28. Mauclair, *Princes de l'Esprit*, p. 114.
29. See Scherer, *Le " Livre " de Mallarmé*, pp. 130-38.
30. Bernard, *op. cit.*, p. 135.
31. "Notes sur le théâtre," *RI*, III (juin 1887), 368.
32. Mallarmé, *Propos sur la poésie*, p. 223. Cf. Noulet, *L'Œuvre poétique de Stéphane Mallarmé*, p. 515.
33. "Notes sur le théâtre," *RI*, I (novembre 1886), 39.
34. *Ibid.*, p. 38. Cf. André Chastel, " Le théâtre est d'essence supérieure," *Les Lettres*, III (1948), 95.

35. "Notes sur le théâtre," *RI*, I (novembre 1886), 40. This view of Hamlet as the sole character in the play is elaborated in Mallarmé's "Hamlet et Fortinbras," *Revue Blanche*, XI (1896), 96, reprinted in *O. c.*, p. 1564.

36. *RI*, I (novembre 1886), 39.

37. Henri de Régnier, "Hamlet et Mallarmé," *MF*, 17 (mars 1896), 292.

38. *O. c.*, p. 1564.

39. Cf. Jacques Robichez, *Le Symbolisme au théâtre* (Paris, 1957), p. 44.

40. *RI*, I (décembre 1886), 246.

41. See Mallarmé's remarks on the performance of Georges Rodenbach's *Le Voile*, May, 1894, in *L'Amitié de Stéphane Mallarmé et de Georges Rodenbach* (Genève, 1949), p. 119.

42. Cf. André Fontainas, *De Stéphane Mallarmé à Paul Valéry* (Paris, 1928), entry for le 24 octobre 1894.

43. *RI*, II (janvier 1887), 58-59.

44. Delfel, *op. cit.*, p. 180.

45. Cf. Michaud, *Mallarmé*, p. 136.

46. For an excellent summary of Mallarmé's theory of the dance, see Deirdre Priddin, *The Art of the Dance in French Literature* (London, 1952), pp. 54-81. Also see André Levinson, "Stéphane Mallarmé, Métaphysicien du Ballet," *Revue Musicale*, 5 (1923), 21-33; Tamara, "Mallarmé et la danse," *Revue du Caire*, 32 (1954), 260-71; Charles Chassé, "Ce que Mallarmé pensait de la danse," *Les Lettres Nouvelles*, 4 (1956), 118-30.

47. *RI*, IV (juillet 1887), 57.

48. *RI*, I (décembre 1886), 246.

49. Cf. Chassé, *op. cit.*, pp. 126-27.

50. "Notes sur le théâtre," *RI*, I (décembre 1886), 250.

51. *Ibid.*, p. 251.

52. Cf. Frédéric Saisset, "Stéphane Mallarmé et les Prêteresses de la Danse," *Archives Internationales de la Danse*, No. 2 (avril 1933), 70-71.

53. Cf. Bernard, *op. cit.*, p. 54.

54. *O. c.*, p. 304. The original text presents some interesting variations. See *RI*, I (décembre 1886), 249.

55. *O. c.*, pp. 307-09. For discussion of Loïe Fuller, see André Levinson, *La Danse au théâtre* (Paris, 1924), pp. 64-66; Priddin, *op. cit.*, pp. 74-75; Chassé, *op. cit.*, pp. 124-25; Frank Kermode, "Poet and Dancer before Diaghilev, *Partisan Review*, 28 (1961), 48-75.

56. Cf. Priddin, *op. cit.*, p. 73.

57. *RI*, II (janvier 1887), 59.

58. André Levinson, "Stéphane Mallarmé, Métaphysicien du Ballet," p. 31.

59. Mallarmé, *Les Noces d'Hérodiade*, p. 93.

60. Cf. Priddin, *op. cit.*, p. 80; Tamara, *op. cit.*, pp. 261-62; Chassé, *op. cit.*, p. 127.
61. See L. J. Austin, " Mallarmé on Music and Letters," *Bulletin of the John Rylands Library*, 42 (1959), 19-39; S. Bernard, *Mallarmé et la Musique*.
62. See Bernard, *op. cit.*, pp. 70-80.
63. Cf. Davies, *Les " Tombeaux " de Mallarmé*, p. 133.
64. Cited by Mondor, *Vie de Mallarmé*, p. 370, n. 1.
65. Cf. Lehmann, *op. cit.*, pp. 150-52.
66. See Mallarmé's letter of March 7, 1885, in Ghil, *op. cit.*, p. 17.
67. See Roger Lhombreaud, "Deux lettres de Mallarmé à Edmund Gosse," *RLC*, 25 (1951), 355-62.
68. *Ibid.*, p. 358.
69. *Corr.*, p. 161.
70. Cf. Winkel, *op. cit.*, pp. 67-71; Bernard, *op. cit.*, p. 130.
71. Lehmann, *op. cit.*, p. 171.
72. Beausire, *op. cit.*, p. 190.
73. Cf. " Notes sur le théâtre," *RI*, II (mars 1887), 389.
74. Cf. Henri de Régnier, " Mallarmé au théâtre," *Journal des Débats*, 7 septembre 1908.
75. André Fontainas, *De Stéphane Mallarmé à Paul Valéry*, entry for le 13 février 1895.
76. *RI*, IV (juillet 1887), 59.
77. *Ibid.*, p. 60. Cf. Bénichou, *op. cit.*, pp. 284-85.

CHAPTER V

1. See *O. c.*, pp. 1563-65.
2. Vittorio Pica included long excerpts from the dialog of Hérodiade and the Nurse in " Les Modernes Byzantins," *RI*, 18 (février 1891), 211-14.
3. Charles Morice, *La Littérature de tout à l'heure* (Paris, 1889), p. 195.
4. *Ibid.*, p. 365.
5. *Ibid.*, p. 240.
6. Gustave Kahn, " Un Théâtre de l'Avenir," *Revue d'Art Dramatique*, 15 (juillet-septembre 1889), 335-53.
7. *Ibid.*, p. 342.
8. Jacques Robichez, "Lugné-Poe, le symbolisme et le théâtre," *La Table Ronde*, No. 127-128 (juillet-août 1958), 117.
9. Cited by Robichez, *Le Symbolisme au théâtre*, p. 184.
10. Pierre Valin, " Le symbol au théâtre," *L'Ermitage*, 3 (janvier 1892), 28-29.
11. Remy de Gourmont, *Le Problème du Style* (Paris, 1924), p. 200.

12. For a general discussion, see Wais, *Mallarmé*, pp. 388-414.
13. Cf. *L'Amitié de Stéphane Mallarmé et de Georges Rodenbach*, p. 102, n.
14. Remy de Gourmont, *Le Problème du Style*, p. 166.
15. Cf. Émile Verhaeren, *Impressions*, troisième série (Paris, 1928), p. 115.
16. Thibaudet, *op. cit.*, p. 464.
17. *Art et critique*, le 4 janvier 1890, cited in Robichez, *Le Symbolisme au théâtre*, p. 81.
18. Cf. Robichez, *op. cit.*, p. 87.
19. *Ibid.*, p. 367.
20. Lugné-Poe, *Le Sot du Tremplin* (Paris, 1930), p. 223.
21. Cf. Robichez, *op. cit.*, pp. 364-67.
22. Lugné-Poe, *op. cit.*, p. 232.
23. Alfred Jarry, "De l'inutilité du théâtre au théâtre," *MF*, 19 (septembre 1896), 472.
24. A.-F. Lugné-Poe, "A Propos de L'Inutilité du théâtre au théâtre," *MF*, 20 (octobre 1896), 93.
25. *Ibid.*, p. 96.
26. *Ibid.*, p. 95.
27. René Lalou, *Le Théâtre en France depuis 1900* (Paris, 1951), p. 40.
28. Cf. Jean-Marie Carré, "Maeterlinck et les Littératures Etrangères," *RLC*, 6 (1926), 449. Also see Jules Huret, *Enquête sur L'Evolution Littéraire* (Paris, 1901), pp. 128-29.
29. Maeterlinck, *Bulles Bleues* (Monaco, 1948), p. 198.
30. Huret, *op. cit.*, p. 128. Cf. Maeterlinck, *Bulles Bleues*, p. 196.
31. Remy de Gourmont asserts that Maeterlinck originally had strong naturalistic leanings, and was directed toward mysticism and "les études d'âme" by Villiers. See *La Belgique Littéraire* (Paris, 1915), p. 112.
32. An exception is A. Jackson Mathews, *La Wallonie* (New York, 1947), pp. 69-70.
33. Cited in Henri Davignon, *Charles Van Lerberghe et ses amis* (Bruxelles, 1952), p. 38.
34. Albert Mockel, "Chronique Littéraire," *La Wallonie*, 4 (1889), 113.
35. Mathews, *op. cit.*, p. 70.
36. Maeterlinck's letter is reprinted in Remy de Gourmont, *La Belgique Littéraire*, pp. 99-102.
37. Davignon, *op. cit.*, p. 38.
38. Cf. R. O. J. Van Nuffel, "Van Lerberghe devant le symbolisme français," in *Les Flandres dans les Mouvements Romantique et Symboliste* (Paris, 1958), pp. 141-44.
39. This is the view of Fernand Séverin, cited by Van Nuffel, *op. cit.*, p. 147.
40. *Ibid.*, p. 141.

41. Davignon, *op. cit.*, p. 158.
42. Verhaeren's review appeared in *Art moderne*, le 21 juillet 1889, and is reprinted in *Impressions*, troisième série, pp. 131-41.
43. Maeterlinck, "Menus Propos: Le Théâtre," *La Jeune Belgique*, 9 (1890), 331.
44. *Ibid.*, p. 335.
45. Huret, *op. cit.*, p. 121.
46. *Ibid.*, pp. 125-26.
47. For the fullest discussion of the subject, see "Mallarmé et Maeterlinck," *Empreintes*, No. 10-11 (septembre-octobre 1952), 96-104. Also see Georges Hermans, "C'est Mallarmé qui *découvrit* Maeterlinck," *Le Livre et l'Estampe*, No. 22 (1960), 138-41.
48. Maeterlinck has recorded his stupefied reactions in *Bulles Bleues*, pp. 203-14.
49. Cf. Mauclair, *Mallarmé chez lui* (Paris, 1935), pp. 43-44; positive evidence is provided in Mondor, *Vie de Mallarmé*, p. 754, n. 4.
50. Maeterlinck, *Bulles Bleues*, p. 208.
51. Cited in *Empreintes*, No. 10-11 (septembre-octobre 1952), 104.
52. *Ibid.*, p. 103. Cf. *Annales de la Fondation Maurice Maeterlinck*, 2 (1956), 58 and n. 1.
53. Cited in Mondor, *Vie de Mallarmé*, p. 590.
54. Cf. Thibaudet, *op. cit.*, pp. 373-74.
55. Mallarmé's letter is dated March 25, 1888 and is reprinted in *L'Amitié de Stéphane Mallarmé et de Georges Rodenbach*, p. 48.
56. An interesting analysis of *La Princesse Maleine* may be found in May Daniels, *The French Drama of the Unspoken* (Edinburgh, 1953), pp. 55-62.
57. Albert Mockel, "Chronique Littéraire," *La Wallonie*, 5 (1890), 207.
58. *Ibid.*, p. 209.
59. Cf. *O. c.*, p. 1569.
60. Cf. Albert Mockel, "Chronique Littéraire," *La Wallonie*, 5 (1890), 216.
61. For a discussion of Vielé-Griffin's relation to symbolist theories and techniques, see J. de Cours, *Francis Vielé-Griffin* (Paris, 1930), p. 172; Guy Michaud, *Message Poétique du Symbolisme* (Paris, 1947), pp. 538-42.
62. The citation from Mallarmé's letter of June 17, 1888 may be found in *Propos sur la Poésie*, p. 161.
63. J. de Cours, *op. cit.*, p. 40.
64. Cf. Robichez, *op. cit.*, p. 195, n. 94.
65. For an emphatic statement of this opposition, see Albert Béguin, "Notes sur Mallarmé et Claudel," *Les Lettres*, III (1948), 205-16.
66. Cf. Ernest Friche, *Etudes Claudéliennes* (Porrentruy, 1943), pp. 143-50; Henri Mondor, "Mallarmé et Paul Claudel," *La Revue*, I (1948),

395-418; A. E. A. Naughton, "Claudel and Mallarmé," *Romanic Review*, 46 (1955), 258-74; Henri Mondor, "Introduction à la Correspondance Claudel-Mallarmé," *Cahiers Paul Claudel*, No. 1 (Paris, 1959), 15-39.

67. Romain Rolland, *Le Cloître de la Rue d'Ulm* (Paris, 1952), p. 281.
68. *Ibid.*, p. 284.
69. Henri Guillemin, *Claudel et son Art d'Ecrire* (Paris, 1955), p. 82.
70. Cited in Friche, *op. cit.*, p. 144.
71. Stéphane Mallarmé-Paul Claudel, "Correspondance" (1891-1897), *Cahiers Paul Claudel*, No. 1 (Paris, 1959), 44-45.
72. Cf. Fernand Vial, "Symbols and Symbolism in Paul Claudel," *Yale French Studies*, No. 9 (1952), 95.
73. Guillemin, *op. cit.*, p. 89.
74. *Ibid.*, p. 96.
75. Cf. Albert-Marie Schmidt, "L'Itinéraire symboliste de Claudel," *La Table Ronde*, No. 88 (1955), 24-26.
76. Jean-Richard Bloch, *Destin du théâtre* (Paris, 1930), p. 113.
77. Henri Mondor, "Introduction à la Correspondance Claudel-Mallarmé," p. 31.
78. Cf. Jacques Madaule, "Un Portrait de Jeune Homme," *Cahiers Renaud-Barrault*, 27 (octobre 1959), 14-15.
79. Jacques Petit has collected the correspondence concerning the play in "Autour de la publication de 'Tête d'Or,'" *Cahiers Paul Claudel*, No. 1 (1959), pp. 135-70. The remarks in the letter to Mockel are to be found on p. 140.
80. *Ibid.*, p. 147.
81. Stéphane Mallarmé-Paul Claudel, "Correspondance," pp. 40-41.
82. "Autour de la publication de 'Tête d'Or,'" p. 140.
83. Cf. Stanislas Fumet, "Claudel lutteur réfléchi," *Cahiers Renaud-Barrault*, No. 27 (octobre 1959), 35.
84. Cited by Henri Mondor, "Introduction à la Correspondance Claudel-Mallarmé," p. 25.
85. Paul Claudel-André Gide, *Correspondance, 1899-1926* (Paris, 1949), p. 199, cited in Roger Bauer, "Paul Claudel et Richard Wagner," *Orbis Litterarum*, 11 (1956), 197.
86. Rolland, *op. cit.*, p. 281.
87. See Claudel's letter to Mallarmé of March 25, 1895, in *Cahiers Paul Claudel*, No. 1 (1959), 43-45. Cf. Guillemin, *op. cit.*, p. 27.
88. Bauer, *op. cit.*, p. 202.
89. See Jean-Louis Barrault, "Du 'Théâtre Total' et de *Christophe Colomb*," *Cahiers de la Compagnie Madeleine Renaud—Jean-Louis Barrault*, No. 1 (1953), 30-41.
90. Cf. Vial, *op. cit.*, pp. 98-102.
91. Cf. Claudel, *Figures et Propositions* (Paris, 1936), p. 203. Also see

J.-R. Bloch, *op. cit.*, pp. 192-93.

92. Claudel, " Un coup d'oeil sur l'âme japonaise," *NRF*, 21 (1923), 391. Cited in Juliette Decreus, " Paul Claudel et le Nô Japonais," *Comparative Literature Studies*, 5th Year, 19 (1946), 12.

93. Friche, *op. cit.*, pp. 147-49.

94. Naughton, *op. cit.*, p. 273.

95. Antoine Orliac, " Henri de Régnier et le Message du Héros," *MF*, 284 (1938), 68.

96. Verhaeren, *Impressions*, troisième série, p. 149.

97. Saint-Antoine, " Le théâtre symboliste," *L'Ermitage*, 5 (septembre 1894), 153.

98. Cf. Robichez, *op. cit.*, p. 322.

99. Cf. Knowles, *op. cit.*, pp. 187-88. Despite Sarcey's hostile remarks, it would seem probable that the riot stemmed from the reactions of supporters of the Théâtre de l'Œuvre to the mutterings of impatience of certain spectators.

100. Henri de Régnier, *Proses datées*, p. 32.

101. See Mallarmé's letter of September 28, 1891 to Alfred Vallette, in *MF*, 298 (1 décembre 1946), 230.

102. See Mallarmé's letter of December 1894, in *L'Amitié de Stéphane Mallarmé et de Georges Rodenbach*, p. 74.

103. See Mallarmé's letter of October 25, 1895, in *Dialogue Stéphane Mallarmé-Francis Jammes, 1893-1897* (La Haye, 1940), p. 30.

104. See Mallarmé's letter of April 1898 to Emile Verhaeren, in *Propos sur la Poésie*, p. 223.

105. For an account of the rupture, see Robichez, *op. cit.*, pp. 393-98.

106. Cited by Robichez, *op. cit.*, pp. 340-41.

107. G. B. Shaw, *Dramatic Opinions and Essays* (New York, 1916), I, 60.

CHAPTER VI

1. Banville, " Préface " of 1874 to *Le Sang de la Coupe*, in *Poésies complètes* (Paris, 1891), III, 282.

2. Jean Cocteau, " Discours sur Mallarmé," *Fontaine*, t. IV, No. 21 (mai 1942), 90.

3. See my essay, " Hugo von Hofmannsthal and the Symbolist Drama," *Transactions of the Wisconsin Academy of Sciences, Arts and Letters*, 48 (1959), 161-78.

4. Cf. Ronald Peacock, *The Poet in the Theatre* (New York, 1946), pp. 117-28. For a provocative evaluation of the symbolist drama, see John Gassner, *Form and Idea in Modern Theatre* (New York, 1956), pp. 97-109.

5. Robichez, *op. cit.*, p. 360.

6. Cf. Mallarmé, " Notes sur le théâtre," *RI*, IV (juillet 1887), 60.

7. Cf. Valéry, " Histoire d'Amphion," *Variété*, III (Paris, 1936), 81-89.

8. Robichez, *op. cit.*, p. 396.

9. Lehmann, *op. cit.*, p. 192.

10. Cf. Kenneth Douglas, " A Note on Mallarmé and the Theatre," *Yale French Studies*, No. 5 (1950), 108-10. Also see the excellent discussion by Wallace Fowlie, " Mallarmé and the Aesthetics of the Theater," in *Dionysus in Paris* (New York, 1960), pp. 265-76.

11. Cited by Jean Royère, *Mallarmé*, p. 44.

BIBLIOGRAPHY

The Bibliography is limited to secondary sources cited in the text

Austin, L. J. "Le 'Cantique de Saint Jean' de Stéphane Mallarmé," *AUMLA*, No. 10 (May, 1959), 46-59.

———. "Le Principal Pilier, Mallarmé, Victor Hugo et Richard Wagner," *Revue d'Histoire Littéraire de la France*, LI (1951), 154-80.

———. "Les Années d'Apprentissage de Stéphane Mallarmé," *Revue d'Histoire Littéraire de la France*, LVI (1956), 65-84.

———. "Mallarmé et le rêve du 'Livre,'" *Mercure de France*, CCCXVII (janvier 1953), 81-108.

———. "Mallarmé on Music and Letters," *Bulletin of the John Rylands Library*, XLII (1959), 19-39.

Baldensperger, Fernand. *Goethe en France.* Paris, 1904.

Barrault, Jean-Louis. "Du 'Théâtre Total' et de *Christophe Colomb,*" *Cahiers de la Compagnie Madeleine Renaud—Jean-Louis Barrault*, I (1953), 30-41.

Bauer, Roger. "Paul Claudel et Richard Wagner," *Orbis Litterarum*, XI (1956), 197-214.

Beausire, Pierre. *Mallarmé: Poésie et Poétique.* Lausanne, 1949.

Béguin, Albert. "Notes sur Mallarmé et Claudel," *Les Lettres*, III (1948), 205-16.

Benda, Julien. "Mallarmé et Wagner," in *Domaine Français*. Genève, 1943, pp. 353-59.

Bénichou, Paul. "Mallarmé et le public," *Cahiers du Sud*, XXX (1949), 272-90.

Bernard, Suzanne. *Mallarmé et la Musique.* Paris, 1959.

Blanchot, Maurice. "L'Expérience d'Igitur," in *L'Espace Littéraire*. Paris, 1955, pp. 108-21.

Bloch, Jean-Richard. *Destin du théâtre.* Paris, 1930.

Block, Haskell M. "Dramatic Values in Mallarmé's *Hérodiade*," in *Stil- und Formprobleme in der Literatur*, ed. Paul Böckmann. Heidelberg, 1959, pp. 351-57.

———. "Hugo von Hofmannsthal and the Symbolist Drama," *Transactions of the Wisconsin Academy of Sciences, Arts and Letters*, XLVIII (1959), 161-78.

———. "Strindberg and the Symbolist Drama," *Modern Drama*, V (1962), 314-22.

Boschot, Adolphe. "Le wagnérisme de Stéphane Mallarmé," *L'Echo de*

Paris, le 4 octobre 1923, p. 4.

Carcassonne, E. "Wagner et Mallarmé," *Revue de Littérature Comparée,* XVI (1936), 347-66.

Carré, Jean-Marie. "Maeterlinck et les littératures étrangères," *Revue de Littérature Comparée,* VI (1926), 449-501.

Castex, P.-G. and Raitt, A. W. "De *Morgane* au *Prétendant,*" in *Autour du Symbolisme,* ed. Pierre-Georges Castex. Paris, 1955, pp. 25-32.

Chassé, Charles. "Ce que Mallarmé pensait de la danse," *Les Lettres Nouvelles,* IV (1956), 118-30.

⸻. "Le thème de Hamlet chez Mallarmé," in *Autour du Symbolisme,* ed. Pierre-Georges Castex. Paris, 1955, pp. 157-69.

Chastel, André. "Le théâtre est d'essence supérieure . . . ," *Les Lettres,* III (1948), 93-105.

Chisholm, A. R. *Towards Hérodiade.* Melbourne, 1934.

Čiževskij, Dmitrij. "Das Buch als Symbol des Kosmos," in *Aus zwei Welten.* The Hague, 1956, pp. 85-114.

Claudel, Paul. "La Catastrophe d'Igitur," *La Nouvelle Revue Française,* XXVII (1926), 531-36.

Cocteau, Jean. "Discours sur Mallarmé," *Fontaine,* t. IV, No. 21 (mai 1942), 88-90.

Cohn, Robert Greer. *L'Œuvre de Mallarmé: Un Coup de Dés.* Paris, 1951.

Contini, Gianfranco. "Sulla trasformazione dell' 'Après-midi d'un Faune,'" *L'Immagine* (Roma), II, No. 9-10 (agosto-dicembre 1948), 502-13.

Cornell, Kenneth. *The Symbolist Movement.* New Haven, 1951.

Cours, J. de. *Francis Vielé-Griffin.* Paris, 1930.

Crépet, E. and J. *Charles Baudelaire.* Paris, 1928.

Curtius, Ernst Robert. "The Book as Symbol," in *European Literature and the Latin Middle Ages.* New York, 1953, pp. 302-47.

Daniels, May. *The French Drama of the Unspoken.* Edinburgh, 1953.

Davies, Gardner. "Introduction" to Mallarmé, *Les Noces d'Hérodiade.* Paris, 1959.

⸻. *Les "Tombeaux" de Mallarmé.* Paris, 1950.

⸻. *Vers une explication rationnelle du 'Coup de Dés.'* Paris, 1953.

Davignon, Henri. *Charles Van Lerberghe et ses amis.* Brussels, 1952.

Decreus, Juliette. "Paul Claudel et le Nô Japonais," *Comparative Literature Studies,* 5th Year, XIX (1946), 11-17.

Delfel, Guy. *L'Esthétique de Stéphane Mallarmé.* Paris, 1951.

Douglas, Kenneth. "A Note on Mallarmé and the Theatre," *Yale French Studies,* No. 5 (1950), 108-10.

Drougard, E. "Richard Wagner et Villiers de l'Isle-Adam," *Revue de Littérature Comparée,* XIV (1934), 297-330.

Dujardin, Edouard. *Mallarmé par un des siens.* Paris, 1936.

Fongaro, Antoine. "L'après-midi d'un Faune et le Second Faust," *Revue des Sciences Humaines*, Fasc. 83 (juillet-septembre 1956), 327-32.

Fontainas, André. *De Stéphane Mallarmé à Paul Valéry*. Paris, 1928.

Fowlie, Wallace. "Mallarmé and the Aesthetics of the Theater," in *Dionysus in Paris*. New York, 1960, pp. 265-76.

——. *Mallarmé*. Chicago, 1953.

Friche, Ernest. *Etudes Claudéliennes*. Porrentruy, 1943.

Fumet, Stanislas. "Claudel lutteur réfléchi," *Cahiers de la Compagnie Madeleine Renaud—Jean-Louis Barrault*, XXVII (octobre 1959), 23-39.

Gassner, John. *Form and Idea in Modern Theatre*. New York, 1956.

Gavelle, Robert. "Goethe et Mallarmé ou les secrets du Faune," *Cahiers du Sud*, XXXIV (1951), 150-54.

Ghil, René. *Les Dates et les Œuvres*. Paris, 1923.

Gill, Austin. "Mallarmé et l'antiquité: L'Après-midi d'un faune," *Cahiers de l'Association Internationale des Etudes Françaises*, X (1958), 158-73.

——. "Le symbole du miroir dans l'œuvre de Mallarmé," *Cahiers de l'Association Internationale des Etudes Françaises*, XI (1959), 159-81.

Gourmont, Remy de. *La Belgique Littéraire*. Paris, 1951.

——. *Le Problème du Style*. Paris, 1924.

Guillemin, Henri. *Claudel et son Art d'Ecrire*. Paris, 1955.

Guyot, Charly. "La genèse de l'Après-midi d'un Faune," in *Stéphane Mallarmé. Essais et témoignages*. Neuchâtel, 1942, pp. 81-106.

Hermans, Georges. "C'est Mallarmé qui *découvrit* Maeterlinck," *Le Livre et l'Estampe*, No. 22 (1960), 138-41.

Jäckel, Kurt. *Richard Wagner in der französischen Literatur*. Breslau, 1931, Bd. 1.

Jean-Aubry, G. *Une Amitié Exemplaire: Villiers de l'Isle-Adam et Stéphane Mallarmé*. Paris, 1942.

Kemp, Robert. *La Vie du Théâtre*. Paris, 1956.

Kermode, Frank. "Poet and Dancer before Diaghilev," *Partisan Review*, XXVIII (1961), 48-75.

Kloss, Erich. "Richard Wagner und die Tanzkunst," *Bühne und Welt*, VII (1904-05), 993-99.

Knowles, Dorothy. *La Réaction Idéaliste au théâtre depuis 1890*. Paris, 1934.

Lalou, René. *Le Théâtre en France depuis 1900*. Paris, 1951.

Lehmann, A. G. *The Symbolist Aesthetic in France*. Oxford, 1950.

Levinson, André. *La Danse au théâtre*. Paris, 1924.

——. "Stéphane Mallarmé, Métaphysicien du Ballet," *Revue Musicale*, V (1923), 21-33.

Lugné-Poe, A.-F. *Le Sot du Tremplin*. Paris, 1930.

Madaule, Jacques. "Un portrait de jeune homme," *Cahiers de la Compagnie Madeleine Renaud—Jean-Louis Barrault*, XXVII (octobre 1959), 3-22.

Margueritte, Paul. " Le printemps tourmenté," *Revue des Deux Mondes,* LI (15 mai 1919), 241-80.

Mathews, A. Jackson. *La Wallonie.* New York, 1947.

Mauclair, Camille. *Princes de l'Esprit.* Paris, 1930.

Michaud, Guy. *Le Message Poétique du Symbolisme.* Paris, 1947.

———. " Le thème du miroir dans le symbolisme français," *Cahiers de l'Association Internationale des Etudes Françaises,* XI (1959), 199-216.

———. *Mallarmé, l'homme et l'œuvre.* Paris, 1953.

Mondor, Henri. *Autres précisions sur Mallarmé et Inédits.* Paris, 1961.

———. *Eugène Lefébure.* Paris, 1951.

———. *Histoire d'un Faune.* Paris, 1948.

———. " Introduction à la Correspondance Claudel-Mallarmé," *Cahiers Paul Claudel,* No. 1 (1959), 15-39.

———. " Mallarmé et Paul Claudel," *La Revue,* I (1948), 395-418.

———. *Mallarmé Lycéen.* Paris, 1954.

———. *Vie de Mallarmé.* Paris, 1941.

Montesquiou, Robert de. *Diptyque de Flandre, Triptyque de France.* Paris, 1921.

Moore, George. *Avowals.* London, 1924.

———. " Souvenir sur Mallarmé," *Parsifal,* No. 3 (1909), 36-37.

Munro, Thomas. " The Afternoon of a Faun and the Interrelation of the Arts," *Journal of Aesthetics and Art Criticism,* X (1951), 95-111.

Naughton, A. E. A. " Claudel and Mallarmé," *Romanic Review,* XLVI (1955), 258-74.

Noël, Jean. " George Moore et Mallarmé," *Revue de Littérature Comparée,* XXXII (1958), 363-76.

Nostrand, Howard Lee. *Le théâtre antique et à l'antique en France de 1840 à 1900.* Paris, 1934.

Noulet, E. *L'Œuvre poétique de Stéphane Mallarmé.* Paris, 1940.

———. " Mallarmé et ' Le Livre,' " *Les Lettres Nouvelles,* V (1957), 334-40.

Orliac, Antoine. " Henri de Régnier et le Message du Héros," *Mercure de France,* CCLXXXIV (1938), 60-91.

———. *Mallarmé: tel qu'en lui-même.* Paris, 1948.

Peacock, Ronald. *The Poet in the Theatre.* New York, 1946.

Priddin, Deirdre. *The Art of the Dance in French Literature.* London, 1952.

Ragusa, Olga. *Mallarmé in Italy.* New York, 1957.

Raitt, A. W. " Autour d'une lettre de Mallarmé," in *Autour du Symbolisme,* ed. Pierre-Georges Castex, Paris, 1955, pp. 141-56.

Régnier, Henri de. *Figures et caractères.* Paris, 1901.

———. " Hamlet et Mallarmé," *Mercure de France,* XVII (mars 1896), 289-92.

———. " Mallarmé au théâtre," *Journal des Débats,* le 7 septembre 1908.

———. *Proses datées*. Paris, 1925.

Robichez, Jacques. *Le Symbolisme au théâtre*. Paris, 1957.

———. "Lugné-Poe, le symbolisme et le théâtre," *La Table Ronde*, No. 127-128 (juillet-août 1958), 116-20.

Rolland, Romain. *Le Cloître de la Rue d'Ulm*. Paris, 1952.

Rougemont, E. de. *Villiers de l'Isle-Adam*. Paris, 1910.

Royère, Jean. *Mallarmé*. Paris, 1931.

Saisset, Frédéric. "Stéphane Mallarmé et les Prêtresses de la Danse," *Archives Internationales de la Danse*, II (avril 1933), 70-71.

Scherer, Jacques. *L'Expression Littéraire dans l'Œuvre de Mallarmé*. Paris, 1947.

———. *Le "Livre" de Mallarmé*. Paris, 1957.

Schmidt, Albert-Marie. "L'Itinéraire symboliste de Paul Claudel," *La Table Ronde*, No. 88 (1955), 24-26.

Shaw, George Bernard. "L'Œuvre," in *Dramatic Opinions and Essays*. New York, 1916, I, 55-63.

Shepard, Odell. *The Lore of the Unicorn*. Boston, 1930.

Souffrin, Eileen. "Coup d'œil sur la Bibliothèque Anglaise de Mallarmé," *Revue de Littérature Comparée*, XXXII (1958), 390-96.

Symons, Arthur. *The Symbolist Movement in Literature*. New York, 1958.

Tamara, "Mallarmé et la danse," *Revue du Caire*, XXXII (1954), 260-71.

Taupin, René. "The Myth of Hamlet in France in Mallarmé's Generation," *Modern Language Quarterly*, XIV (1953), 432-47.

Thibaudet, Albert. *La Poésie de Stéphane Mallarmé*. Paris, 1926.

Valéry, Paul. *Œuvres*. Paris, 1957, t. I.

Van Nuffel, R. O. J. "Van Lerberghe devant le symbolisme français," in *Les Flandres dans les Mouvements Romantique et Symboliste*. Paris, 1958, pp. 138-48.

Verhaeren, Emile. *Impressions*, troisième série. Paris, 1928.

Vial, Fernand. "Symbols and Symbolism in Paul Claudel," *Yale French Studies*, No. 9 (1952), 93-102.

Vivier, Robert. "La Victoire de Mallarmé," *Empreintes*, No. 5 (1948), 90-93.

———. "Mallarmé le Parnassien," *Cahiers du Nord*, XXI (1948), 195-207.

Wais, Kurt. "Die Szenenfolge von Mallarmés Syrinx-Drama und die Hirtentragödie Aubanels," in *Französische Marksteine von Racine bis Saint-John Perse*. Berlin, 1958, pp. 278-306.

———. *Mallarmé*. München, 1952.

Winkel, Joseph. *Mallarmé-Wagner-Wagnerismus*. Bückeburg, 1935.

Wyzewska, Isabelle. *La Revue wagnérienne*. Paris, 1934.

INDEX

Allegory: in Banville, 72; and symbol, 111; in Claudel, 122
Appia, Adolphe, 13
Aubanel, Théodore, 17, 22, 52-53
—*Lou Pastre*, 25
Augier, Emile, 43

Ballet: in Mallarmé and Wagner, 65-67, 94. *See also* Dance
Balzac, Honoré de, 54
Banville, Théodore de, 7-8, 10-11, 21-27, 31-33, 42, 43, 55, 58, 70-75, 81, 83, 86, 89, 106, 129
—*Diane au Bois*, 8, 24-25, 71; *Le Forgeron*, 70-73, 78, 90; *La Pomme*, 72
Barrault, Jean-Louis, 120
Baudelaire, Charles, 7, 54, 55, 60, 62, 107, 132; on Wagner, 80; and *correspondances*, 88
—*L'Art Romantique*, 56-57; *Les Fleurs du Mal*, 56
Beckett, Samuel, 131
Beethoven, Ludwig van, 62, 65
Bernhardt, Sarah, 43
Blaze de Bury, Henri, 26, 45
Bloch, Jean-Richard, 120
Bonniot, Edmond, 37, 38, 47
Byron, George Gordon, 89

Calderón de la Barca, Pedro, 120
Carlyle, Thomas, 107
Cazalis, Henri, 9, 29, 30, 37, 42, 53
Chamberlain, Houston Stewart, 59
Character: in symbolist drama, 45, 132
Chénier, André, 6
Claudel, Paul, 34, 38, 104, 105, 117, 126, 128; and Mallarmé, 118-21;

and symbolist drama, 118-25; and Wagner, 122-23; and Nō drama, 123-24
—*Christophe Colomb*, 123; *Le Soulier de Satin*, 124; *Tête-d'Or*, 120-22, 124; *La Ville*, 124
Cocteau, Jean, 130
Coquelin, Constant, 11, 22, 23, 31, 32, 47
Corneille, Pierre, 100
Craig, Edward Gordon, 13

Dance, 101, 103; in *Hérodiade*, 19; in Wagner, 65-67; in Mallarmé, 65, 93-96
Daudet, Alphonse, 43
Davies, Gardner, 18
Debussy, Claude, 97
Deman, Edmond, 33
De Quincey, Thomas, 91
Des Essarts, Emmanuel, 22
Detheatricalization: in *Hérodiade*, 19; in *Hamlet*, 44-45; in Mallarmé's dramatic theory, 88-89, 92, 94-95, 104-06; at Théâtre de l'Œuvre, 105-06
Dialog: in symbolist drama, 18, 89, 100, 126
Drama: and ritual, 49, 58, 60, 63, 68-69, 71, 73, 76, 78, 85-89, 95, 99, 106, 123-24; and the audience, 60, 73-74, 78-79, 86-87; and poetry, 62, 88, 129-30, 133. *See also* Liturgical drama; Poetic drama
Dramatic ode, 33, 70-71, 75, 90, 93, 99
Dujardin, Edouard, 59, 60, 62, 66, 74, 77, 80, 110; on Wagner, 80
Dumas fils, Alexandre, 20, 43, 84

Emerson, Ralph Waldo, 107

Fort, Paul, 105
Fuller, Loïe, 95

García Lorca, Federico, 131
Gautier, Judith, 56
Gautier, Théophile, 84
Ghelderode, Michel de, 131
Ghil, René, 77, 97
Gide, André, 104, 117, 128
Glatigny, Albert, 7
Goethe, Johann Wolfgang von, 7,
   26, 73, 81, 111
—Faust, 25-26, 30, 31, 44, 47, 54
Gosse, Edmund, 97
Gourmont, Remy de, 20, 104

Halévy, Ludovic, 43
Hegel, Georg Wilhelm, 53-54
Hellenism: in nineteenth-century
   drama, 24, 26, 72, 117, 119
Hofmannsthal, Hugo von, 21, 34,
   116, 131
Hugo, Victor, 7, 20, 26
—Le Satyre, 25; Théâtre en Liberté,
   90
Huret, Jules, 76, 87, 110, 125
Huysmans, Joris-Karl, 17

Ibsen, Henrik, 105, 127
Internalization of dramatic action:
   in Wagner, 62, 66, 68; in Banville, 71-72; in Mallarmé, 88-90,
   102; in Maeterlinck, 112; in Vielé-
   Griffin, 117; in Claudel, 121-22;
   in Régnier, 125-26
Interrelation of the arts: and correspondances, 57-58, 104; in the
   theater, 61, 63; in Wagner, 66,
   79, 102; in Mallarmé, 69, 79-81,
   94, 101, 104; in Claudel, 122-24

Jammes, Francis, 117, 127, 128

Kahn, Gustave, 103-04

Laforgue, Jules, 107
Lamartine, Alphonse-Marie de, 26
Lamb, Charles, 110
Leconte de Lisle, Charles-Marie, 6,
   24
Lefébure, Eugène, 22, 23, 30, 36
Liturgical drama, 58, 73, 85-88, 99,
   120, 123, 132
Lugné-Poe, Aurélien: and the
   Théâtre de l'Œuvre, 105, 127;
   and Mallarmé, 105-06; his view
   of theater, 106; and Maeterlinck,
   107; and Régnier, 126; and the
   symbolists, 127
Lyric drama, 21, 50, 126, 131, 133

Maeterlinck, Maurice, 21, 34, 78,
   104-05, 126, 128; and symbolist
   drama, 107-16; his dramatic
   theory, 110; and Claudel, 121-22
—Les Aveugles, 108, 113; L'Intruse,
   108, 113; Pelléas et Mélisande,
   115; La Princesse Maleine, 105,
   111, 113; Les Sept Princesses, 113-
   14; Serres Chaudes, 109
Mallarmé, Geneviève, 73
Mallarmé, Stéphane, his impact on
   drama, 5, 21, 34, 101-02, 104-05,
   116-17, 126-28, 129-34; his interest
   in theater, 6-7, 42, 43, 73-74, 83-
   84, 92, 100, 129-30; his role in
   the symbolist movement, 6, 104;
   as a dramatic poet, 7, 16, 31-32,
   34, 53; and Shakespeare, 7, 25,
   38, 44, 47-48, 81, 86, 90-92, 114-15,
   120; and Banville, 7-8, 10-11, 21-
   27, 31-33, 42-43, 48, 55, 70-75,
   81, 86, 90, 129; and French classical drama, 9, 34, 55; his dramatic projects, 10-11, 22-23, 33,
   42-43, 45, 48-51, 53, 74-75; his
   doctrine of effects, 11-12, 20; and

music, 12, 61-62, 96-99; his disdain for the theater, 17, 43, 44, 67, 88-89, 92; and theory of genres, 24, 50-51, 81, 94; and cosmic drama, 26, 30, 38, 44, 54, 73, 88; his concept of the artist, 30; his image of Hamlet, 38-39, 41, 44-45, 47, 90-91, 132; existential values in, 40-41; and dramatic realism, 43-44, 70, 83-84; his view of the poet as actor, 46-47, 78, 89-90; and popular theater, 48, 51; his debt to Wagner, 49, 54-75, 79-81; and Hegel, 53-54; and occultism, 54, 75, 77, 88; and the interrelation of the arts, 58, 61-64, 69, 70-71, 75, 79, 93, 96; his ritualistic theory of drama, 60-61, 73, 76, 85-88; his definition of poetry, 60; his criticism of Wagner, 61-68, 96; and the dance, 65-67, 93-96; and Zola, 70, 84; his notion of intimate theater, 74, 78-79, 127; on the social function of drama, 86-87; his concept of *mystère*, 87-88; and static drama, 90; on tragedy, 90-91; and the language of drama, 96-100; and Lugné-Poe, 105-06; and open-air theater, 106; and Van Lerberghe, 109; and Maeterlinck, 109-16; and Claudel, 118-21, 124; and Régnier, 125-26

—*L'Après-midi d'un Faune*, 6, 22, 32, 33; *Autobiographie*, 75-76; *L'Azur*, 7; *Un Coup de Dés*, 76, 98; *Crayonné au Théâtre*, 101; *La Dernière Mode*, 25, 43; *Divagations*, 83, 101; *Le Faune*, 11, 21-35, 55, 72, 88, 106, 129, 130; *La Fausse Entrée des Sorcières dans ' Macbeth,'* 92; *Le Guignon*, 44; *Hamlet and the Wind*, 45-49, 51; *Hérésies Artistiques: L'Art pour Tous*, 55; *Hérodiade*, 7-21, 32-35, 53, 55, 96, 98, 102, 105, 128, 129, 130, 131; *Hommage à Wagner*, 64, 67; *Igitur*, 37-42, 45, 47-48, 54, 87; *Le Livre*, 47, 63, 68, 75-81, 88, 92-93, 96-97; *Loeda*, 6, 7, 24; *Monologue d'un Faune*, 23; *Monologue de Pathelin*, 74; *La Musique et les Lettres*, 97; *Le Mystère dans les Lettres*, 88; *Les Noces d'Hérodiade*, 18-20; *Notes sur le théâtre*, 83; *L'Œuvre*, 20, 27, 36, 41, 50, 52-54, 58, 68, 75-81; *Pages*, 33, 101; *Le Pitre châtié*, 47; *Le Réveil du Faune*, 23; *Richard Wagner: Rêverie d'un poëte français*, 59-64, 67, 80; *Symphonie Littéraire*, 7, 8, 10

Manet, Edouard, 45
Margueritte, Paul, 73-74, 78
Margueritte, Victor, 73
Mauclair, Camille, 68, 104, 110
Meilhac, Henri, 43
Mendès, Catulle, 37, 42, 56-57
Merrill, Stuart, 127
Mirbeau, Octave: on Maeterlinck, 111; on Claudel, 121
Mockel, Albert, 108, 111-13, 120-22
Montégut, Emile, 44
Montesquiou, Robert de, 15, 16
Moore, George, 45-49, 79
—*Avowals*, 47
Morice, Charles, 103
Mounet-Sully, Jean, 84
Music: and poetry, 61, 81, 96-99, 103, 123; and drama, 66-71, 98-99, 115, 123, 126, 132
Musset, Alfred de, 7, 26, 74, 102
—*Un Spectacle dans un fauteuil*, 73
Mysticism: in Mallarmé, 54, 75-76, 80, 88, 99, 102, 104; in Maeterlinck, 110-14; in symbolist drama, 131-32

Nijinsky, Vaslav, 33
Noulet, Emilie, 10
Novalis, pseud. of Georg Friedrich von Hardenberg, 107

Opera: and drama, 55, 63, 69-71, 81, 98, 114, 126
Orfer, Léo d', 60
O'Shaughnessy, Arthur, 48-50

Payne, John, 57
Pica, Vittorio, 65, 76-77
Poe, Edgar Allan, 12, 49-50, 56, 107, 108, 132
Poetic drama, 11, 16, 18, 20-21, 24, 31-32, 51, 69-71, 81, 84, 93, 114, 117, 124, 126, 130-31; language of, 24, 34, 98, 100, 102, 112, 130

Quinet, Edgar, 26

Racine, Jean, 100, 117
Régnier, Henri de, 37, 61, 77, 104-05, 114, 117, 128; on Mallarmé, 86; and symbolist drama, 125-26
—La Gardienne, 106, 125-26
Retté, Adolphe, 105
Robichez, Jacques, 105
Rodenbach, Georges, 68, 104, 112, 116, 127, 128
Rolland, Romain, 118, 123

Saint-Pol-Roux, pseud. of Paul Roux, 117, 128
Sand, George, 26
—Lélia, 25
Sardou, Victorien, 20, 43, 84, 133
Scherer, Jacques, 77
Schuré, Eduard, 56
Scribe, Eugène, 42, 78, 84, 133
Shakespeare, William, 7, 20, 25, 38, 44, 47-48, 65, 73, 81, 86, 90-92, 110-11, 114-15, 120
—Hamlet, 31, 38, 39, 41, 44-45, 47, 54, 84, 90-91, 101, 114, 132; King Lear, 114; Macbeth, 13, 44, 91-92
Shaw, George Bernard, 128
Shelley, Percy Bysshe, 89
Strindberg, August, 34, 131
Swedenborg, Emanuel, 107
Swinburne, Algernon Charles, 49, 89
Symbolist drama: technique of, 34, 63, 71-72, 113, 121; premises of, 85-88, 102-05, 130-32; in the theater, 105, 108, 120, 126-28, 133; achievement of, 125, 127-28, 131-34
Symbolist poetics: 6, 30, 72, 110, 119; concept of suggestiveness in, 99, 113-15, 119, 125-26, 131-32
Symons, Arthur, 55

Théâtre d'Art, 32, 33, 105, 126
Théâtre de l'Œuvre, 32, 118, 128
Thibaudet, Albert, 6, 10, 105
Tragedy: Mallarmé's theory of, 90-91

Valéry, Paul, 68, 104, 117; on symbolist drama, 132
—La Jeune Parque, 15
Valin, Pierre, 104
Van Lerberghe, Charles, 105, 108, 111, 116, 128
—Les Flaireurs, 108-09
Verhaeren, Emile, 104-05, 110, 116, 125, 127, 128
—Les Aubes, 90
Verlaine, Paul, 17, 58, 75, 76, 107, 110, 112
Vielé-Griffin, Francis, 77, 104, 105, 114, 128; and symbolist drama, 117-18
—Ancaeus, 105, 117; Phocas le jardinier, 117-18
Villiers de l'Isle-Adam, Auguste, 7, 21, 26, 34, 36-37, 54, 56-58, 60,

102, 107, 116, 118
—*Axël*, 41, 107, 116, 117; *Elën*, 17, 25, 27, 36, 44, 47, 54; *Isis*, 8; *Morgane*, 36; *La Révolte*, 42

Wagner, Richard, 83, 86, 97-98, 101, 115, 120, 126; and Mallarmé, 49, 54-75, 79-81; and the interrelation of the arts, 50, 67; his impact in France, 54-59, 80, 103, 117, 123; and Baudelaire, 56-58; and Villiers de l'Isle-Adam, 56-57; and the dance, 64-67, 94; and Claudel, 122-23

—*Beethoven*, 62, 68; *Lettre sur la Musique*, 57, 59, 62, 65; *Parsifal*, 66; *Rienzi*, 66; *Tannhäuser*, 25, 66; *Tristan und Isolde*, 62, 117
Whitman, Sarah Helen, 49-50
Wilde, Oscar, 19
Wyzewa, Théodore de, 59, 62, 68, 110

Yeats, William Butler, 21, 34, 79, 116, 123, 131

Zola, Emile, 43, 84, 86
—*Messidor*, 70

The manuscript was edited by Patricia Davis. The book was designed by S. R. Tenenbaum. The text was set in Linotype Janson cut by Mergenthaler Linotype in 1932, and based on a face cut by Nicholas Kis, Amsterdam, 1690. The display faces are Venus cut by Bauer, 1907-13 and Delphian designed by R. H. Middleton for Ludlow, 1930.

The book is printed on Olde Style Antique paper from the S. D. Warren Co. and bound in Strathmore Cover. Manufactured in the United States.